PRAISE FOR *WELCOME TO THE JUNGLE*

"Hilary Smith has come through big time with a book about bipolar disorder targeted to teens or 20-somethings experiencing mental illness for the first time."
—*Washington Post*

"Hilary Smith's *Welcome to the Jungle* provides readers with wise and excellent counsel about the thing called bipolar disorder. At once radical education and exuberant conversation, this combo memoir and self-help book is a must read for the millions whose ups and downs cause them to collide with psychiatry and the current supremely flawed mental health system."
—Eric Maisel, PhD, author of *The Future of Mental Health* and *Rethinking Depression*

"*Welcome to the Jungle* does an excellent job of distilling important and trustworthy information. Hilary Smith strikes an effective balance in addressing the experience of bipolar teens and young adults who are struggling to come to terms with the reality of their illness. What they'll find in Ms. Smith's writing is sensible information from someone who talks their talk and walks with balance gained from her own personal journey."
—Russ Federman, PhD, ABPP, psychologist, author, and blogger: *Bipolar You* in *Psychology Today*

"An edgy and informative account. Refreshingly, Hilary Smith manages to bring humor into the discussion of an illness that is often written of only in somber terms. While recognizing the challenges inherent in bipolar disorder, she poses an optimistic outlook with her exploration of "jungle wanderers." The upbeat tone of *Welcome to the Jungle* is most welcome!"

—Stephanie Marohn, author of *The Natural Medicine Guide to Bipolar Disorder*

"Hilary Smith brings to light what those with bipolar already know: that just because you've been diagnosed with a mental illness doesn't mean you've lost your insight, intelligence, or playful (and often self-mocking) sense of humor. *Welcome to the Jungle* astutely captures the roller coaster of emotions that accompany bipolar—from trenchant despair to uproarious mania— and does so in a way that never alienates the reader, but rather sucks you in and keeps you wanting to go along for the ride. Writing with a wisdom and faculty well beyond her years, Smith had me laughing out loud—not at her, but with her. Whether you're a teen for whom the diagnosis of bipolar is as raw and fresh as a snipped nerve, or in your twenties struggling with the disease for what seems like decades, *Welcome to the Jungle* is the quintessential young person's companion."

—Malina Saval, author of *The Secret Lives of Boys: Inside the Raw Emotional World of Male Teens*

"Hilary Smith's wise, hilarious, and candid book is a veritable lifesaver not only for those suffering from bipolar disorder, but for those struggling to keep their sanity while loving them. Maybe because the author suffers from the disorder herself, her book is an actual survival guide, brimming with insight, anecdote, and tough love. Recovery was never so inspiring."

—Allison Burnett, author of *Undiscovered Gyrl*

"By far the best, most comprehensive self-help book out there about bipolar disorder. Hilary Smith's incredible sense of humor, candor, and wit make her guide easy to read, a pleasure, and a laugh riot. Every person with bipolar (or family member or friend) should read this book as soon as possible. This book will save lives."

—Andy Behrman, author of *Electroboy: A Memoir of Mania*

"Funny, smart, and unflinchingly astute, *Welcome to the Jungle* is exactly the guide you want on your journey from chaos to stability as you learn to manage bipolar disorder. Smith's sure voice is a welcome companion over some hard road, and her wry wisdom lights the way. Indispensable."

—Marya Hornbacher, author of *Madness: A Bipolar Life* and *Wasted: A Memoir of Anorexia and Bulimia*

HILARY SMITH

WELCOME TO THE JUNGLE

REVISED EDITION

FACING BIPOLAR WITHOUT FREAKING OUT

Conari Press

This edition first published in 2017 by Conari Press, an imprint of
Red Wheel/Weiser, LLC
With offices at:
65 Parker Street, Suite 7
Newburyport, MA 01950
www.redwheelweiser.com

ISBN: 978-1-57324-695-8

Library of Congress Cataloging-in-Publication Data
Smith, Hilary, 1986–
  Welcome to the jungle : everything you ever wanted to know
about bipolar but were too freaked out to ask / Hilary Smith.
      p. cm.
  ISBN 978-1-57324-472-5 (alk. paper)
  1. Depression in adolescence—Popular works. 2. Manic-
depressive illness in adolescence—Popular works. 3. Smith,
Hilary, 1986—Health. 4. Manic-depressive illness in adoles-
cence—Patients—Canada—Biography. I.
Title.
  RJ506.D4S585 2010
  616.85'2700835—dc22

                          2009050798

Cover design by Jim Warner
Text design by Jane Hagaman
Typeset in ITC New Baskerville and Toronto Gothic

Printed in Canada
MAR
10 9 8 7 6 5 4 3 2 1

CONTENTS

INTRODUCTION TO THE 2017 EDITION

When my publisher contacted me about doing a second edition of this book, I felt a little bit like a punk musician being asked to go on a promotional tour for a rerelease of an album she'd recorded when she was still playing reggae at bar mitzvahs: "I can't put on those old clothes and go sing those old songs—I'm a different person now! It would be a lie—a reggae-flavored act of deception!" But the more I thought about it, the more I came around to the idea. What if I didn't have to wear a dreadlock wig and play the same four chords on my old synthesizer? What if I could play the tour as myself—a wizened thirty-year old with slightly different insights and ideas than the fresh-faced youth I was back then? What if, rather than pretending the intervening seven years hadn't happened, I used my experiences and insights to make the original act way better than it had been before?

That's when I started to get really excited.

I wrote the first edition of *Welcome to the Jungle* when I was twenty-three. At the time, I was less than two years out of college, living with roommates and just starting out as a writer. Bipolar was very much at the forefront of my mind, since I had only been diagnosed a few years before. My imagination was completely enchanted by the idea of being mentally ill—a status that seemed both crippling and darkly glamorous (all my favorite writers and musicians were manic-depressive; now I was in the club, and I had to admit it felt a little bit cool.)

Since then, my thinking on what we call mental illness has evolved quite a bit. I have had a lot more time to observe myself; to see for myself whether my own lived experience matched up with the bipolar prophecy read out by the doctor ("Thou shalt have manic episodes and depressive episodes of ever-increasing intensity! Thou shalt never live another day without meds!") and to realize the many ways in which it very strongly diverges. It has been a priority for me in this revised edition to emphasize the many, *many* paths that people diagnosed with mental illness can take in life. Every person is different, and this is just as true for people with a mental illness diagnosis as for people without.

Over the years, I've also grown more and more uncomfortable with the way our medical system pathologizes human experience. Not all weeping is depression; not all dancing is mania—yet if you take the *Diagnostic and Statistical Manual of Mental Disorders* too seriously, you just might start to believe that, relegating all sorts of important and meaningful aspects of life to the category of "I'm just bipolar and need my meds adjusted." To tell you the truth, it's been years since I've even thought of myself as being "bipolar." I am not "bipolar"; I am human. (Does that disqualify me from writing this book? Or am I more qualified than before? I hope you will agree that it is the latter.)

With that in mind, this new edition has a greater focus on the human, not the diagnosis: the ways in which each person can find his or her own way through the extreme emotional states and intense experiences that we are calling "bipolar"—whether that means medication or meditation, psychiatrists or vision quests, good sleep or good all-night dancing, or a little bit of everything.

Sincerely,
Hilary

INTRODUCTION TO THE 2010 EDITION

This is a book about bipolar disorder. Or if you're a free spirit or an R. D. Laing enthusiast who doesn't believe in a pathological explanation of your extreme mood states, it's a book about living with the highs and lows everyone *else* in North America is calling "bipolar disorder" (the punks!). I'm supposed to use this introduction to tell you my personal story about having bipolar, but that can wait.

Right now I've got a hankering to write about shin splints.

I got shin splints when I was thirteen. They hurt. My Anglophilic boarding school made everyone participate in enforced jaunty after-school sports (and, every spring, supposedly jaunty sniper drills on the lawn). After a single week on the cross-country running team, jogging along behind the meaty-calved senior boys, my shins started to feel weird. Little shoots of pain sprang up each time my shoes hit the pavement. It really hurt, but I winced and kept running. If I ignored the problem, it would probably fix itself. Four practices went by. I limped along. During the fifth practice the coach (of whom I was terrified) rode up behind me on a bicycle and shouted, "Stop running! You're limping! Go to the infirmary!"

Confused and embarrassed, but relieved, I turned around and walked to the school physiotherapist's office, where a team of smokin' hot sports therapists treated me for shin splints. Going to physio was fun and cool: there were always tons of people there getting their ankles wrapped or their sprains ultrasounded, or just hanging out in the whirlpool drinking from sketchy-looking Nalgene bottles. The physiotherapists teased me about letting my shin splints get so bad without asking for help. I did the stretches and exercises, got a better pair of running shoes, and eventually started running again.

Total days of pain: less than five.

Social approval of shin splints: high.

Overall experience with shin-splints diagnosis and treatment: supercool!

Six years later, I was a junior at the University of British Columbia, majoring in English literature. No more sports, no more sniper drills. This was the West Coast, baby—poetry readings, pot, and rainy-night house parties. I lived in a funky old house in Kitsilano that had a rich history of student debauchery and was known to several generations of UBC students as the place to go for anything involving mint juleps and knife throwing. Six of us lived there, and it got *loud.*

In January of that year, I started having trouble sleeping. Writing it off to the constant noise and stimulation in the house, I didn't pay much attention. By February I couldn't sleep at all, and my mind was swimming in thoughts and rhymes. Box! Fox! Haha!

In lectures, I either scribbled furiously in the diary I carried with me everywhere, recording my urgent insights ("He was an ornithologist. He was bornithologist into it!"), or I stood up abruptly to leave partway through and weep in the bathroom or wander in the forest that surrounded the campus. At parties, I would give my phone number to several different guys, then panic and jog home through the night, all the way from East Van to Kitsilano. At my part-time job as a bagel-stand cashier, I would prop my ever-present diary over the cash register and worry about the people who came to buy bagels: whether they knew what I was thinking, if they might be interested in coming to a fabulous party I was planning. At night, I would lie down in bed as a formality, then spring back up ten minutes later when sleeping didn't work out. Eventually, the mental chatter in my mind intensified so much that it felt like there were "four of me" whose constant arguments and repartees were alternatingly sinister and hilarious.

It really hurt, but I winced and kept going. If I ignored it, it would probably fix itself. Time passed. I limped along. Even though whatever was wrong with me was more pronounced than a physical limp and should have been more obvious, there was no coach to ride past on a bicycle and shout, "Stop running!"

So I didn't.

I felt like a ceiling light whose switch was stuck in the on position. Whatever I did, I couldn't turn myself off. Confused and tormented by my condition, I nevertheless strode through the days, handing in essays, going on dates, and calling my parents long distance for normal, how's-the-weather conversations. Even though I was falling apart inside my head, I wasn't *doing* anything that had enough obvious craziness to attract anyone's attention. Not running down the street in my underwear. Not trying to convince the bank teller I was Jesus. Just wandering around having thoughts that went off like sparklers and a body that had forgotten how to fall asleep.

When I finally went to see a doctor at the walk-in clinic down the street, it wasn't because I wanted to help myself or because I thought I might have a medical disorder. It was out of shame. I had started crying and rambling in front of my roommates one night because I couldn't sleep, and I felt so embarrassed for crying in front of them that I was determined to get sleeping pills so it wouldn't happen again. I waited in the exam room, feeling guilty for taking up the doctor's time when there were three-year-olds with runny noses waiting to be seen, and when the doctor came in, I started crying all over again. When she asked what was wrong, I blurted, "I can't do this anymore!"

That's when someone finally said, "Stop running."

Over the next few weeks, I went through the usual mental-illness maze of being misdiagnosed with unipolar depression, becoming hypomanic (again) from antidepressants, being rediagnosed with bipolar II, and choking down a series of different antipsychotics and mood stabilizers until I hit on a combination that didn't make me want to bury myself in a hole. I spent a lot of time in the waiting room of the UBC hospital, which was neither fun nor cool, because everyone there either had an STD or a mental illness and there was no freaking whirlpool.

Total days of pain: lots and lots.

Social approval of bipolar: not obvious.

Overall experience with bipolar diagnosis: kinda really bad.

My dad flew out from Ontario to see how I was doing and make sure I wasn't completely crazy. We blasted through the Chapters bookstore in downtown Vancouver, and he bought me every bipolar-related book on the shelf. We made a stop at the Starbucks. As we were power walking down the street, my dad hailed a taxi midsentence, hopped in, and rushed off to catch his flight back to Ontario. I stood on the sidewalk with a bag of bipolar books in one hand and a half-finished Green Tea Frappucino in the other.

The party was just getting started.

In the days that followed, I returned most of the bipolar books and used the money to buy poetry books—not because I wasn't interested in the former, but because they made me feel tainted and messed up. They were too adult, too clinical, too alarmist, clearly written for family and caretakers at their wits' end, and designed to look authoritative and medical. They didn't answer any of the questions I had about bipolar, and I felt like a huge tool for even having them in my room, their ALL CAPS titles blaring out at the world. I thought there should be a book that was a little more honest, a little more badass, and a little more sympathetic to the average teen or twenty-something's first experience of the mental-health system.

So here's that book.

This book is mainly about how to live with bipolar, but it's also about how to *think* about bipolar. Sure, you can think of bipolar as a chemical imbalance in your brain, but you can also imagine it as a video game, a shamanic journey, a crash course in existentialism, or a plain old pain in the ass.

If you're reading this book and you've just been diagnosed with bipolar disorder: welcome to the jungle. Hope you brought bug spray, 'cause the spiders in here are as big as your face. Taken your meds? Good.

Now let's get started.

WHAT JUST HAPPENED?
LIFE BEYOND THE DIAGNOSIS

How did it happen?

Maybe you were doing a research project on the Beatles, and by the end of the term you thought you were one of the Beatles. Maybe you were trying to find a girlfriend, and at the end of a futile year of looking you were trying to die. Maybe you were having a perfectly happy summer that turned into an ecstatic summer or a winter sadness that never lifted when spring came. The sun was shining, cars were honking, the radio was playing something catchy. You were toasting a bagel, playing Xbox, talking to your best friend about the afterlife, or tuning your guitar.

Then the mothership landed.

You were diagnosed with bipolar disorder. This big whale of a diagnosis slid over the sun, and your world was suddenly held hostage. A hatch slid open and out came doctors, psychiatrists, pills, hospitals, and self-help books. They strapped you to a gurney and scrawled "bipolar" on your chest in permanent marker. "I'm not bipolar!" you shouted, struggling in your restraints. "She's bipolar! He's bipolar! Anyone but me!" They gave you two Depakote and a glass of water. "Misdiagnosed!" you snarled, gulping it down.

Eventually, the mothership flew away, but left its cargo behind. Medication, doctors, and bipolar were seemingly here to stay. You picked your way out of the rubble, the last one standing after an earth-shattering encounter. Your ray gun is strapped to your side;your freshly acquired jar of anti-psychotics and mood stabilizers is on your other hip. You step out of the doctor's office.

WHAT JUST HAPPENED?

Dealing with a bipolar diagnosis can be just as hard as the unfettered depressive or manic episodes that led up to it. It's like you've been hit by a truck, only to be told at the scene of the accident that you're going to be hit by several more trucks of steadily increasing size over the course of your life (have fun with that). For a while, it's hard to think about anything else but the fact that you're screwy enough to be considered mentally ill, and especially hard to accept a diagnosis of mental illness if you've always considered yourself a happy, healthy person. The diagnosis looms over your life, and you just want to rewind to a time before it happened. *Can anything be the same again? How did they even decide I have bipolar?*

Being told you have a serious mental illness is a colossal mind fuck. In fact, some doctors and psychiatrists are now questioning whether it's even a good idea to tell people they have a "serious lifelong mental illness" when they experience something that looks like mania or depression. Why? Because having an authority figure like a doctor inform you that you are "mentally ill" gives you certain expectations ("I'm going to be unstable and need meds my whole life!") that can actually make it harder for you to recover. The label of bipolar disorder can lead you to reinterpret your life in a certain way, giving special importance to mood while downplaying things like relationships, family dynamics, your ability to find meaning in life (or lack thereof) and various kinds of trauma which can play an equally large role in your ability to cope with life. What does "bipolar" even mean? And what does it really say about who you are? This chapter is about understanding what the people in white coats were thinking when they made the diagnosis. Even if you hate everything to do with jargon and psychiatry and labels like "bipolar," you should know this stuff so you understand what (and who) you're dealing with.

WHAT IS BIPOLAR, ANYWAY?

Asking "What is bipolar?" is a little bit like asking "What is Christmas?" On the one hand, pretty much everyone thinks they "know" what Christmas is—yet if you asked ten different people, you'd get ten different answers: "Christmas is a Christian holy day celebrating Jesus's birthday." "Christmas is a consumer holiday about buying stuff." "Christmas is a pagan winter solstice festival co-opted by Christianity."

You figure out pretty quickly that "Christmas" is not something that exists independently of people's ideas and fantasies: there's no scientific test for Christmas ("ah, there are ten units of Christmas in the air today!"). On the contrary, Christmas is an idea; a thing that's real because a bunch of people have agreed to talk about it a certain way and accord it a certain structure (Christmas *always* has a tree and a snowman, even if the snowman is made of plastic).

In this sense, bipolar disorder is a little like Christmas. It's an idea—an idea with lots of research and science and history backing it up (just like Christmas!) but also a construct dreamed up by our culture's medical system and influenced by very specific cultural values and assumptions. (Up until very recently in human history, they didn't have "bipolar" in Egypt or Samoa or Belize any more than they had "Christmas"—they are both *ideas* that got exported; interpretations of reality, not scientific facts.)

So before we get into *anything* involving mania or depression or any of those things you expect to find in a book about bipolar, please review the following reminder: "Bipolar" is a word.

It is a word psychiatrists made up so they would have a way to bill insurance companies. Insurance companies won't reimburse psychiatrists for treating suffering, but they will reimburse them for treating "bipolar."

It is a word psychiatrists made up because it is easier to give patients medication for "bipolar" than to say "you are suffering and I think this pill might help." People in our culture are uncomfortable taking a pill because it will help them feel better (it feels like cheating), but we're OK with taking a pill if it's treating an identifiable and socially validated disease.

It is a word psychiatrists made up because it would take too long at psychiatry conventions if everyone talked about "my patient who is really sad but also agitated and also can't sleep and also sleeps too much and also drinks too much and also can't quite hold down a job and is also a genius at painting and also had a terrible childhood"— it's more convenient to say "bipolar."

It is a word our culture uses because we're comfortable with medical problems, and definitely *not* comfortable with problems that imply there is anything wrong with our social and economic systems. It is easier to say, "You have bipolar!" than to say "The modern world demands people to be rigid and efficient, ambitious and desensitized, and if you are not those things, you're going to have a very hard time."

It is a word our culture uses because we are comfortable with medical problems, and definitely not comfortable with spiritual experiences. It is easier to say, "You are psychotic!" than to entertain the possibility that someone really did see God, or levitate, or have a profound insight into the Kabbalah, or whatever.

This is not to say that bipolar is a meaningless word or an arbitrary word or a word some kooky psychiatrist cooked up just for the hell of it—but all words have limits, and when we're talking about a word as powerful as bipolar, it's essential to keep an eye on the context.

"WHY ARE YOU HARPING ON THIS STUFF, YOU WIZENED OLD HAG?"

Because it's true, and it's important. Yes, this book is going to talk about bipolar disorder in the "normal" sense (in the very next paragraph, in fact!) But if you don't understand the social and cultural context of this diagnosis, you're missing a whole lot.

BIPOLAR? SAYS WHO?

There are four things a psychiatrist takes into account before making a diagnosis of bipolar disorder: your current symptoms, your medical history, your family history, and your psychiatric history. Doctors see hundreds and hundreds of people and know what to look for. They look for patterns ("Wow, that guy talks in a constant stream without any pauses, and he hasn't slept for a week. And his uncle has bipolar, and he's taken four jobs") that are consistent with what we're calling bipolar. You, of course, are a beautiful and unique snowflake, but like it or not, there are a number of classic behaviors and indicators (big and small) that people experiencing mania, hypomania, or depression in our culture tend to present. Quibble over details all you like, but if the shoe fits in five places, they're sticking that sucker on your foot. P.S. Hope you like Velcro.

THINGS THAT GO INTO A BIPOLAR DIAGNOSIS

1. CURRENT SYMPTOMS

Do you *seem* depressed or manic? Have you mentioned being unable to sleep, unable to think straight, or crying all the time? Are you talking fast? Of course, *you* may feel that you are acting normally, but it can be very hard to reflect accurately on yourself especially if your symptoms have been creeping up on you over weeks or months. Over time, a psychiatrist will be able to compare your "manic" or "depressed" behaviors to your "baseline." (For example, the psychiatrist might figure out that you *always* talk fast. It's just who you are, no big deal.) But for a first diagnosis, the only thing they can really compare you to is the general population.

2. MEDICAL HISTORY

Do you have another disease, like epilepsy or diabetes, that might be causing your symptoms? Are you on crack? Pregnant? On the autism spectrum? Have a brain tumor? Or are you just hungry? Many medical conditions share symptoms with bipolar. You want to rule these out as possible causes before deciding the diagnosis is bipolar.

Of course, it can be difficult to rule out other conditions if those conditions are undiagnosed (maybe nobody's realized you're autistic, or pregnant, or anorexic, or have some obscure vitamin deficiency that is either causing or exacerbating your "bipolar" symptoms) or if those conditions are not recognized by your culture as being valid (like having a spiritual awakening or emergency.)

Unless you're on a really cushy medical plan, it's unlikely your doctor will run the dozens of tests necessary to exhaustively rule out other possible causes for your distress. It is therefore important to take as thorough an inventory as possible of your own health *before* you go to your doctor's office. Write down a year-by-year health inventory, as far back as you can remember. Include anything that seems significant, whether or not it seems relevant to "mental" health (after all, physical health and mental health are closely entwined). Have you ever had seizures? Insomnia? Childhood anxiety or depression? Self-mutilation? Stress-related conditions like eczema? Had a traumatic injury that still causes you pain? Other chronic illnesses? Frequent fevers or flus?

This might all seem a little over-the-top, but the more of an expert you can become on the working of your own mind and body, the happier you will be in the long run. Even if the doctor looks over the list and decides your symptoms are still mostly due to bipolar (even though you do have anemia and PTSD and a few other things with bipolar-esque symptoms), the inventory can help you see the bigger picture and help you come up with a plan to improve your overall health, not just the "bipolar" part of you. Mind and body are related—a fact which gets over-looked too easily in the drama of a mental illness diagnosis.

CONDITIONS THAT SHARE SYMPTOMS WITH BIPOLAR

Believe it or not, bipolar disorder doesn't have the market cornered on things like insomnia, grandiosity, and suicidality. Here are just a handful of conditions that share these symptoms:

Condition: Aspergers/Autism Spectrum Disorder
Bipolar-esque features: Depression, anxiety, obsessions, socially inappropriate behavior, periods of intensely focused activity, social burnout and withdrawal, loneliness, hypersensitivity, suicide attempts, seeming "grandiosity."

Condition: Temporal Lobe Epilepsy
Bipolar-esque features: Bouts of paranoia and confusion, overwhelming ecstatic/spiritual experiences, depression, hallucinations.

Condition: Anxiety Disorders
Bipolar-esque features: Paranoia, panic, restlessness, obsessions, fear, worry, insomnia, depression, strange behaviors, self-medicating with alcohol/drugs.

Condition: Primary Insomnia
Bipolar-esque features: Inability to sleep with seemingly no cause; can lead to hallucinations, agitation, depression, suicidality, self-medicating with drugs/alcohol.

Condition: Chronic pain
Bipolar-esque features: Depression, suicidality, insomnia, anxiety, self-medicating with drugs/alcohol.

Condition: Seasonal Affective Disorder
Bipolar-esque features: Marked changes in mood and energy levels, insomnia, anxiety, hypersensitivity.

Condition: Spiritual Experience
Bipolar-esque features: Intense energy, feeling like God or talking to God, seeing lights and colors, "grandiosity,"

desire to talk to strangers or make big gestures. Other times: depression, suicidality, guilt, agitation, dissociation. (People on meditation retreats experience this stuff all the time.)

"OH MY GOD, I THINK I HAVE ALL OF THESE! I'M AN ASPIEBIPOEPIANXIOUSPAINSOMNIAC—*AND* I'M ALLERGIC TO KIWIS, CAT HAIR, AND RAIN!"

OK, OK, easy, Tiger. You might be an AspieBipoEpi-AnxiousPainSomniac . . . or you might just be a human being who's working with a particularly challenging mind and body, the same way your cousin Angie is a human being who's been working on an unusually challenging muscle car for the past six years (she got it running ages ago, but now she's obsessed with getting it to make a particularly . . . *muscular* . . . kind of roar when it drifts around corners . . .).

On the other hand, AspieBipoEpiAnxiousWhat-ever might not be that far off the mark. With the rise of genetic testing, scientists are finding possible links between conditions like bipolar, autism, and schizophrenia—hinting that they might not be as separate and distinct as we've assumed. Other researchers have found a strong connection between bipolar disorder and chronic pain, bipolar and anxiety, bipolar and trauma, bipolar and Kundalini syndrome (it's a thing!). . . the list goes on. So where does one condition end and the next one begin? It's hard, if not impossible, to pinpoint. That's why it's important to take steps that improve your whole life, not just "bipolar"—because "bipolar" is almost never the whole story.

3. FAMILY HISTORY

It's taken as a given that your uncle Bernie is off his rocker, but has anyone else in your family been diagnosed with a mental illness? Have any of your relatives been hospitalized for depression, mania, or psychosis? Anyone receiving counseling or taking meds for a psychiatric disorder? Or does anyone have a condition that can look similar to bipolar, such as Aspergers, temporal lobe epilepsy, schizophrenia, or straight-up depression? Bipolar appears to have a strong genetic component, and bipolar in the family can predict bipolar in you. Don't be afraid to contact family members and relatives to get as complete a picture as possible. Maybe your mom/uncle/grandpa has a condition you didn't even know about.

4. PSYCHIATRIC HISTORY

Did you get diagnosed with unipolar depression three months ago, and now you have so much energy you can't sleep? Have you ever been diagnosed with another psychiatric disorder? The doctor will want to rule out unipolar depression, schizophrenia, and other possible psychiatric causes for your symptoms. The doctor might ask you to draw a "mood chart" of the past twelve months or several years. This might seem obvious, but if you've been through a recent trauma such as rape, a violent relationship, or even a scary car accident, you should definitely speak up. Trauma can shake you up in a way that resembles mental illness. And if you have both a mental illness and trauma, there's no reason you should address only one of the two and ignore the other.

You didn't get diagnosed with bipolar because you're ugly or because the doctor doesn't like you. Let's face it—he's uglier, and his personality needs improving. You got diagnosed bipolar because your symptoms more or less fall into a common, distinct pattern, observed in millions of people. We're currently calling that pattern "bipolar" and treating it with pharmaceuticals and talk therapy. In the past, the same pattern has been called by a different name (hello, "hysteria") and treated by different means (like lots of cold showers). In the future, it will undoubtedly be called something else entirely and treated with mind melding and cosmic nanoprobes. In other cultures, what we call "bipolar" has other names and other symptoms and explanations entirely.

No matter what the psychiatric community wants to call it, you're still you—whether you have bipolar, hysteria, a wandering womb, or just plain sand madness. Everybody else changes their mind about what to call it, so there's no reason why you can't too. Don't think "bipolar" is an accurate description of your experience? How about Chronic Sleep Taxationitis or Acute Porn Star Overidentification Syndrome? No matter what you call it, no matter how you think about it, no matter how you treat it, you're a person—not a collection of symptoms or an entry in the *DSM-V* (the hefty diagnostic manual produced by the American Psychiatric Association that you've probably seen lurking under your psychiatrist's desk). Nothing can change that. Don't dwell on whether or not "bipolar" is the perfect way of describing your condition; actually, dwell as much as you'd like, but do consider whether the solutions available for bipolar are helpful for you.

And in the year 2037, when they yank "bipolar" from the *DSM-XXIV* and replace it with "Intergalactic Hypersensitivity Disorder," you can go through the whole ride all over again ("Intergalactic Hypersensitivity Disorder—it explains everything about me, man . . . now pass the nanoprobes!")

Life is long, and your understanding of yourself (not to mention your family, your culture, and your weird roommate Sun Man) can and should evolve over time. It's OK to go through many stages with your thoughts and feelings about bipolar disorder. Who knows—in the course of your wanderings, you might just hit on something useful or wise.

WHY DO I HAVE BIPOLAR?

WHY DID I GET BIPOLAR?

This is a really, *really* great question, and you'll get a lot of different answers depending on who you ask:

Psychiatrist: "You have bipolar because you have bipolar genes and your brain chemistry is out of whack."

Anti-psychiatrist: "The whole 'brain chemistry' thing has no proven scientific basis, and it's mostly a play by the pharmaceutical industry and the American Psychiatric Association to get more and more people on meds."

Sociologist: "You were diagnosed with bipolar because you come from a certain socioeconomic class and a certain culture, you live in a certain society at a certain time, and the beliefs of your society cause people like you to be labeled 'bipolar.'"

Therapist: "You had a traumatic childhood, as did your parents and grandparents, and it was easier for society to label you as 'mentally ill' than to take responsibility and address the root causes of your ongoing distress."

Ecopsychologist: "We have poisoned the earth, deleted meaningful social roles, and broken down tribal and family structures. Of course you're freaking out. And of course they're going to blame it on your 'brain chemistry.'"

Scientist: "No really, it's totally genes and brain chemistry. We've studied the hell out of this shit. Don't listen to those hippies."

As you can see, there are a lot of different opinions about what constitutes 'bipolar disorder' and what causes 'it' to manifest in a given person. And you can find intelligent, reasonable, highly qualified people to argue every one of those positions.

As far as I'm concerned, there is at least a grain of truth in all of these arguments—they're not necessarily mutually exclusive. The pattern we call bipolar seems to have a genetic component *and* a trauma component *and* a social component *and* a cultural component and

an environmental component, and—sure, why not?—
an astrological component and a yogic component and
a Star Wars use-the-force component and who knows
what else.

My point in bringing all this up is not to sow unnecessary confusion or to undermine any particular group's
point of view. On the contrary: I think the more angles
from which you approach your own mental health, the
better. If you attribute all your ill-health to brain chemistry and treat it with only medication, you might neglect
to address your physical health, your emotional life, your
relationships, your beliefs, and other factors that have a
very real impact on your overall wellness. If you attribute
all your ill-health to social and environmental factors,
and treat it with *only* lifestyle changes and talk therapy,
you may have your progress interrupted by a manic episode that could have been easily prevented with a touch
of lithium.

Every person is different, and every person diagnosed
with bipolar is different. Sometimes I wonder if the thing
we call bipolar has different causes for different people: if
some people have "classic" bipolar, which is truly genetic,
neurochemical, and lifelong, and some people have
more of a situational bipolar disorder—a response to chaotic surroundings, housing instability, poor coping skills,
or trauma, which is more environmental than genetic
in nature. This could account for why some people with
bipolar ardently praise medication, and some people also
diagnosed with bipolar seem to do better with therapy,
meditation and lifestyle changes. Of course, there are
also those people who seem to do best with both!

People who have been diagnosed with bipolar always have a certain narrative about how it developed: "I'd just gotten my first job and my first girlfriend, my parents divorced, and I started going crazy." "I was staying up late, listening to a lot of Marilyn Manson, and shit just started getting weirder and weirder." For one thing, humans love to tell stories. It makes much more sense to place bipolar disorder in the context of certain events, rather than having it come out of nowhere. Though the environmental triggers of bipolar disorder are not well understood, one thing many accounts have in common is a period of lifestyle change, stress, or major life events (both positive and negative). Real specific, huh? Try naming a time in your teens and twenties when you're *not* going through a period of stress, lifestyle change, or major life events!

In other cultures, narratives of mental illness sometimes focus on spiritual matters ("he is being haunted by ghosts!") or family relations rather than biochemistry. Our Western narrative might be scientifically accurate, but it is not necessarily the most useful or compassionate way of imagining mental illness. If "haunted by ghosts" feels more meaningful and accurate to you than "haunted by misbehaving neurotransmitters," then please, tell your own story!

Otherwise, it's you against the mothership. Lock and load, lock and load. . . .

EIGHT WAYS TO PROVE YOU DON'T HAVE BIPOLAR

1. Keep a straight face and neutral affect at all times. This will demonstrate how completely stable your mood is.

2. Whenever you hear something about bipolar disorder on the news, laugh loudly and say, "Ho, ho, ho, I'm so perfectly twitterpated to not be affected by such a foreign and fearsome affliction as that!"

3. Paint rabbit faces on your meds so they look like recreational drugs. Wear furry clothing and plastic beads so people think you're a raver.

4. When you get hospitalized, tell everyone you know you're an "investigative journalist" doing an exposé of what it's "really like" to be hospitalized.

5. Hire a look-alike to impersonate you at social events when you're too depressed to go out.

6. Surround yourself with people who are more extreme than you (drama students, nonrecovering addicts, circus people). In contrast, you will look totally un-bipolar.

7. Start a fake blog about your completely normal, nonbipolar life. Include entries such as, "Fun day at the mall!" and "New kitty is cute!"

8. Get a high-powered career that could never be held by a person with a mental illness. That will show them!

WELCOME TO THE JUNGLE

2

MANIA, DEPRESSION, PSYCHOSIS, OH MY!
A WHIRLWIND TOUR THROUGH
THE EPISODES OF BIPOLAR DISORDER

States of human experience are extremely difficult to classify. Where does a mood end and a physical sensation begin? Where does a mental experience end and a spiritual experience begin? What's the difference between a bad mood and a bad day? Are some days just inherently sad or manic, or are "sad" and "manic" things that only happen inside individual people, and not in groups of people or in the wider world? Can a person be "depressed" or "manic" in a vacuum, or are those states in constant interplay with other people in the outside world?

Are you still "manic" if you feel really sad while you rearrange your furniture at three in the morning? Are you still "depressed" if you have two really bad days, then three really great ones, then two bad ones again? Is it still "psychosis" if you perceive your experience to be the result of intense yoga practice? Is it still "depression" if you have lots of energy and will to live, but feel overwhelming grief that they drained your favorite swamp to build a shopping mall?

These are all questions the *Diagnostic and Statistical Manual of Mental Disorders* (the book psychiatrists use to diagnose mental illnesses) does not get into. The *DSM* is all about putting human experiences into categories—drawing lines even where it doesn't make sense to draw them.

Think about a tree in the forest. It has bark and leaves and branches, which are obviously part of the tree. But what about the moss growing on the bark, and the ferns growing on the branches, and the mycelium intertwining with the roots, and the insects nesting in the wood? Are they part of the tree? Are they separate? Are they somewhere in between? A claim in either direction is very much up for debate. (The tree would die if you stripped off all the moss, or killed the mycelium—then again, can you really say that moss is *part* of a tree?)

Mood descriptions are no different. Take depression, for example. There's a feeling of sadness and a physical heaviness which are "obviously" part of being depressed. But your knee hurts from where you tore your meniscus, your job is entering data into a computer all day, and you hear cars and trucks driving past your house all the time, and you feel really, really down about that swamp. Are the cars and the job and the swamp part of your depression? Or is the feeling of sadness and the heaviness in your body the only part of depression that counts?

In this chapter, I am going to go through the *DSM* definitions of bipolar mania, depression, and psychosis because you are probably going to Google them anyway (don't lie!). But listen to me: even if some aspects of these descriptions sound familiar to you, don't let them overwrite the details of your personal experience. It's easy to read this stuff and say, "Oh yeah, I guess my mood lasted for four to seven days, and come to think of it, I *did* sleep less that month," even when that isn't the whole story. There's a strong human impulse to identify with categories (that's why people get so obsessed with their astrological signs). At its worst extreme, the *DSM* can act as a script for "how to be bipolar" even if that's not how you experienced your moods before getting diagnosed.

So please keep perspective as you read this. Even if the *DSM* description of bipolar sounds *just like you,* don't lose sight of the moss and ferns and all the other unique details that make you *you.*

I'M NOT MANIC, I'M JUST HYPHY

Before we get into all this bipolar stuff, let's talk about hyphy. Hyphy is a Bay Area hip-hop style characterized by people dancing or acting in a hyperactive, ridiculous manner. You put on your stunna shades, get blasted, and "go stupid." One particularly prestigious way of "going stupid" is to put your car in neutral and dance on the hood while it rolls forward without a driver; this is called ghost-riding the whip. E-40 and Mistah F.A.B. wrote entire songs about ghostin'.

Now, when you think about it, all this going stupid sounds a lot like a manic episode: substance abuse, hyperactive speech and dancing, risky and grandiose activity—feelin' like a star. Yet thousands of otherwise sane, asymptomatic people get hyphy every day, and nobody accuses them of having bipolar disorder. What's the difference between being manic and plain old gettin' hyphy?

MISTAH F.A.B.'S GUIDE TO THE *DSM-V*

Hyphy	"Dude, Bro, let's ghost-ride your car then put it on YouTube, Bro, ha ha ha. Babes will dig it. Wooooo!"
Hypomanic	"Dude, bro, stop the car, we're going to ghost-ride the whip right-now. Yeah yeah, stop the car. We need to do it right now right now right now, ha ha ha!"
Manic	"I *am* Mistah F. A. B. I'm the hyphiest motherfucking ghost-rider in West Oak. I'm gonna buy this Lexus with my credit card and ghost-ride *that*."
Psychotic	"A tribe of angels is watching me ghost-ride the whip, and Satan is broadcasting the lyrics to *Ghost-Ride It* directly into my brain."
Unhyphy	"Dude, I just wanna park somewhere and get a Slurpee."
Depressed	"Watching YouTube videos of people ghostin' makes me incredibly sad."
Hella Depressed	"I haven't gotten out of bed in a week because all I can think about is how horrible my life is compared to Mistah F. A. B.'s."
Suicidal	"I've said goodbye to my family and friends and am actively seeking out people to roll their car over me as they dance on the hood."

As you can see, there's a broad behavioral spectrum to ghost-riding the whip, and in this case, I've categorized behaviors as "manic" or "depressed" based on how far they deviate from the hypothetical Mistah F.A.B.'s normal hyphy or unhyphy mood states. In the following section, I'm going to be discussing the criteria physicians use to identify the different aspects of bipolar disorder as outlined in the *DSM-V*, that big fat book published by the American Psychiatric Association that contains the diagnostic criteria for all the psychiatric disorders our society currently believes in. Like the songs in a jukebox, the stock of "mental disorders" in the *DSM* changes all the time—up until 1973, homosexuality was listed as a mental disorder (message to APA pre-1973: you guys aren't doing your credibility any favors . . .) It hardly needs saying that the *DSM-V* is not a perfect guide to mental illness, and that some of the "illnesses" that have been described there in the past are no longer considered illnesses at all. Unlike pregnancy, you can't pee on a stick to find out if you have bipolar disorder. Definitions evolve over time, and in a hundred years, the category "bipolar disorder" might be as antiquated as the category "hysteria" is today. The purpose of the following section is to discuss the common symptoms of mania, hypomania, and depression and what they can feel like—and also to help you resist the urge to dump every experience in your life into one of those categories.

NORMAL HAPPINESS AND NORMAL ENERGY—HUZZAH!

When you've just been diagnosed with a major disorder like bipolar, you might have the urge to reinterpret *every-thing* in terms of either mania/hypomania or depression. But honestly, not every moment in your life is depressed or manic: much of the time, you're just plain old you. Normal happiness and energy are just that—*normal*. You don't need to pathologize your enthusiasm for flying kites or attribute your last romantic success to hypomania. You're probably a charming, loveable, energetic person in "real life"—good for you! You can be ambitious, adventurous, and fun loving outside of mania. The key difference between a "normal" state and a manic or hypomanic state is whether or not your perceptions of reality and your own abilities have shifted, and whether this shift messes up your ability to relate to other people or get your work done. If you're normally a beast on the dance floor who loves to hook up with hot strangers, good for you! If you're a lifelong wallflower who is suddenly electrified with the belief that you're Justin Timberlake bringing sexxy back—well, maybe that's not normal. Let's be perfectly clear: you're allowed to grow and change, try new things, whatever. If done with a clear mind, almost any action you undertake can be considered normal. You should worry about it only if you start basing your actions on unusual logic or logic radically different than your default setting, or if people around you start noticing a marked departure from your usual behavior.

Going skydiving because you think it's cool = normal. Going skydiving *because you temporarily believe you're an invincible god* = not normal. Being a talkative person = normal. All your friends are staring at you because you've been talking like an auctioneer all day = not normal.

MANIA

All ghostin' aside, what is mania, and how can you or other people tell if you're manic? You're manic if your belief about your own capacities expands drastically, if you start engaging in activities that are drastically out of character, making plans drastically out of sync with reality, or behaving in an overblown, irrational, out-of-control manner. It can be hard for *you* to tell if you're manic, at least immediately, but it's pretty easy for other people to tell. You think you're a celebrity, believe you can walk in front of traffic, and obsessively call the Federal Reserve to tell them your brilliant solution to the economic recession. You feel like you don't need to eat or sleep, and feel a vast and potent connection to complete strangers. Words tumble out of your mouth in a great flood. You start taking your job as a mall cop too seriously and stay up all night drafting a new and improved plan for mall safety, which you work on tirelessly with no breaks for several days. *It's the key, the key. People spend all their time in malls, right? Safety is key, right? Mall safety, that's where it's at, that's where it's at.* Your friends and family notice a difference and try to talk you down. "Dear, can we not talk about the menace of escalators tonight?"

Technically, mania is defined by the *DSM-V* as "a distinct period of abnormally and persistently elevated, expansive, or irritable mood, lasting at least one week (or any duration if hospitalization is necessary)." Therefore, drinking too much coffee and running around like a ferret for *one* day doesn't qualify as a manic episode (unless you get caught by animal control and hospitalized for it).

The *DSM-V* lists seven symptoms of mania, at least four of which are usually present in a full-blown manic episode:[1]

1. *Inflated self-esteem or grandiosity*

   You (mistakenly) think you're famous and important or think you have special powers. You suddenly realize you're a better painter than anyone else in your art class, and start plotting an elaborate gallery opening at the Museum of Modern Art, featuring your work next to Van Gogh's. Your teacher is confused because this represents a major change from your normally humble personality.

2. *Decreased need for sleep*

   You keep coming home from the bar at 3 a.m. Tonight you take a one-hour nap, then go for a run, paint the house, and organize a dinner party for all your friends. Sleep is a bad word.

3. *More talkative than usual*

   You have pressured speech (the sensation that you need to be talking) and a flood of ideas you need to express. Friends and teachers ask you to slow down and explain your thoughts, but it's too hard.

4. *Flight of ideas, racing thoughts*

   Your mind is like a speeding train, or several speeding trains on different tracks. You can't slow down your thoughts, and your ideas fly to their wildest conclusions. You might enjoy the sensation of being flooded with ideas at first, but later become overwhelmed and terrified by it.

5. *Distractibility*

   What?

6. *Increase in goal-setting activity or psychomotor agitation*

   You're working on a very important project and realize there are three other side projects you should be doing to really get it off the ground. You check twenty books out of the library and start researching every aspect of your subject

---

1 *DSM-V* (American Psychiatric Association, 2013).

area. You don't understand why other people can't see the importance of your project. You feel the need to move around a lot.

7. *Excessive involvement in pleasurable activities (such as buying sprees, sexual indiscretions, or foolish business investments)*

   You run to the bar and make out with three different people over the course of a Rihanna single. You buy everyone a round, then flag down a taxi and give the driver a $100 tip for driving you home. You want to buy expensive presents for everybody you know.

The *DSM-V* definition goes on to state that the above symptoms should not be the result of illegal drugs and must be severe enough to really wreak havoc on your normal life. Psychosis is sometimes a feature of manic episodes, too.

Everyone's experience of mania is different. Some people experience it as a fabulous period of elation, while other people get extremely agitated and experience no pleasure at all. Mania is on a continuum—it takes your normal behaviors and personality and amplifies them. A manic episode can lead to hospitalization or self-harm, and the tomfoolery you get up to while manic can demolish your savings, land you in prison, and make you feel embarrassed later on. Mania can also give you a unique drive and a window into realms of the mind that are inaccessible to most people. In other cultures, mania might be given a different name and be seen as a religious experience. The important thing isn't definitions, which change over time, but *effects*, which vary from person to person. For some people, mania has the effect of a revelation or mystical experience, while for others it only causes misery.

PUTTING IT ALL TOGETHER

Here's how mania might look. The numbers below refer to the symptoms listed on pages 26 and 27.

Let's say you work at a call center for IBM. You spend all day on the phone to customers, helping them fix their computer problems. You're also in charge of logging their questions and complaints in a database. Over the course of a week, you start to notice connections between calls that you never noticed before (4). You realize there's a pattern to the database that could revolutionize the future of IBM (1). You start staying at the office long past closing time, working on solving this pattern far into the wee hours (6). Solving the pattern is more important than eating or sleeping (2). When you tell your coworkers and supervisors about the pattern you discovered, they seem confused, though you talk about it incessantly (3). You get frustrated because nobody else can see how important and revolutionary your discovery is. Even your girlfriend doesn't understand your great discovery, but she wants you to tell Dr. Brunner about it because she thinks she will.

HYPOMANIA

For hypomania, take the mania section and turn the volume down several notches. You talk faster, walk faster, and think faster—enough for other people to comment. Maybe you start writing a novel, building a sailboat, and recording an electro album all on the same day. Or you join a rock-climbing gym because you "suddenly" realize you'd make a fabulous rock climber. It's hard to sleep and hard to sit still and listen when someone else is talking. Other people seem to be talking and moving incredibly slowly. Sitting in class is torture because it seems to drag on for hours and hours, and you've got more important things to do! You might be agitated and elated at the same time, the life of the party, but your engine's running a little hot. You dance down the street, filled with this wonderful sense of how happy the world is, or flit around your room like a trapped fly.

The *DSM-V* definition of hypomania includes the same seven symptoms as for mania, but the difference is that the episode is not severe enough to land you in the hospital or make it impossible for you to get through a normal day at work or school. It also notes that a change in your mood and behavior should be observable to other people (i.e., that your parents or friends notice that you're talking faster and making uncharacteristic judgments). A hypomanic episode marks a distinct change from your usual self, and the elevated, expansive, or irritated mood should last for at least four days. Hypomania usually isn't accompanied by psychosis, and it doesn't count (at least, not to the guy in the white coat) if your symptoms are due to your taking a drug like ecstasy.

Hypomania can imbue you with wonderful feelings of confidence, talent, creativity, self-esteem, charm, and intelligence, all of which can help you achieve great things. It can also feel distinctly uncomfortable and irritating—sometimes both at once.

HOW MIGHT MY FRIENDS REACT
TO MANIA OR HYPOMANIA?

A good way to gauge whether or not you're acting abnormally is to pay attention to your friends' and family's reactions. Sometimes, nobody will realize you're manic until it's too late. But people who know you can usually sense when something is a little off. From a friend's perspective, your "perfectly reasonable" obsession with the pattern in the IBM call database is *not* perfectly reasonable. A friend can have good insight even when you've lost it. Here are some comments friends might make if you're acting unusually.

> "You're acting really intense."
> "You've been working on that project nonstop for a week. Don't you ever sleep?"
> "Are you high?"
> "What are you talking about? You're not the CEO of Microsoft!"
> "Slow down, you're not making sense."
> "Are you drunk?"

If friends *know* you have a bipolar diagnosis, they might give feedback like:

> "You're getting a bit speedy."
> "Have you been sleeping?"
> "This is really out of character for you."

It can be really annoying to hear these comments, especially if you feel strongly that you're *not* manic or hypomanic. But it's worth being patient with them, because a trusted friend's insight can help you rein in your energy before it gets out of hand.

DEPRESSION AND SADNESS: WHAT'S THE DIFF?

A bunch of nerds had a conference in Las Vegas. After enjoying steak and strippers (male strippers! lots of male strippers!), they defined clinical depression as having a handful of symptoms that persist for at least two weeks and represent a change from your regular functioning. If you've experienced depression, you can probably list the symptoms yourself: a sad, depressed mood for most of the day; a loss of pleasure in activities you normally like; changes in eating and sleeping; crying a lot; fatigue; recurring thoughts of death. At the extreme, people can become catatonically depressed: too depressed to move or speak. The symptoms of depression overlap with conditions such as vitamin deficiencies and chronic fatigue. So it's important for doctors to rule out other factors when making a diagnosis. Unfortunately, many people with bipolar disorder experience more depressive episodes than manic or hypomanic episodes in their lifetime. How do doctors differentiate between depression and normal sadness or grief? Back to the *DSM-V!*

1. *Depressed mood most of the day, nearly every day, as indicated by either subjective report (e.g., feels sad or empty) or observation made by others (e.g., appears tearful)*

You feel sad, down, and empty. Maybe you cry a lot. This feeling persists from day to day.

2. *Markedly diminished interest or pleasure in all, or almost all, activities most of the day, nearly every day (as indicated by either subjective account or observation made by others)*

   You don't feel like going out with friends, doing your laundry, calling your girlfriend, or going to the gym. Activities you normally enjoy feel sad or painful to you.

3. *Significant weight loss when not dieting or weight gain (e.g., a change of more than 5 percent of body weight in a month), or a decrease or increase in appetite nearly every day*

   You find it hard to eat, or you eat a whole box of ice cream just to distract yourself from the sadness. Your body feels strange and makes different hunger demands than usual.

4. *Insomnia or hypersomnia nearly every day*

   You have a terrible time getting or staying asleep at night. Or all you want to do is sleep—you start sleeping twelve hours a day, every day.

5. *Psychomotor agitation or retardation nearly every day (observable by others, no merely subjective feelings of restlessness or being slowed down)*

   You look and feel like you're moving through molasses. It takes you thirty seconds to take your bowl of oatmeal out of the microwave. Your friends get impatient because it takes you forever to put on your jacket. Or you feel agitated and move around like an angry old man.

6. *Fatigue or loss of energy nearly every day*

   You dread the time between periods when you have to walk from one lecture hall to the other. You feel really tired—too tired to do the things you normally do.

7. *Feelings of worthlessness or excessive or inappropriate guilt (which may be delusional) nearly every day (not merely self-reproach or guilt about being sick)*

   You feel extremely guilty about being a terrible friend or being a bad person, for no apparent reason. You feel like you have no worth as a person.

8. *Diminished ability to think or concentrate, or indecisiveness, nearly every day (either by subjective account or as observed by others)*

You can't make decisions or prioritize tasks. Thinking about whether to go to the bank or the library first nearly kills you. You can't concentrate on a dinner menu, let alone your thesis.

9. *Recurrent thoughts of death (not just fear of dying), recurrent suicidal ideation without a specific plan, or a suicide attempt or a specific plan for committing suicide*

You can't stop thinking about all things death related. Even if you don't want to commit suicide, you can't stop thinking about how you would do it.

The *DSM-V* goes on to note the same "ruling-out" clauses as for mania and hypomania: that your symptoms aren't better accounted for by drug abuse, a medical condition like hyperthyroidism or chronic fatigue, or bereavement following the death of a loved one. The depressive symptoms must represent a marked change from your regular functioning and persist over at least two weeks.

The key words are "change from your regular functioning" and "persistent." If you feel like the world has become inherently more depressing and your prospects in life fundamentally bleaker—and these feelings last for a long time and deplete your functioning—it might be depression. If you're just having a bad day and temporarily feel down on yourself, it's probably run-of-the-mill sadness. If you're just not hungry one day, it's probably nothing. But if you lose all desire to eat, have sex, or go outside for two weeks, that's depression. Sometimes you might have a couple days of real depressive symptoms, but manage to pull yourself up before they develop into full-blown depression (tips on doing that later!). In some ways, depression is like the common cold: you can feel it coming on and try to stop it from developing if you catch the symptoms early enough. But once it sinks its teeth in, it can stick around for a long time.

Just like mania, depression can make you do stupid things. On one end of the spectrum, there's suicide, which we'll talk about later. Way on the other end of the spectrum are the stupid thoughts you have when you're depressed. One time when I was depressed, I burst into tears at the sight of a normal white fence and insisted to my boyfriend that it was the saddest fence I'd ever seen in my life. (If you want to see the world's saddest fence for yourself, it's located at 2761 West Seventh Avenue in Vancouver, British Columbia.) Depression can also lead you to lash out at people around you, make poor decisions, and sabotage your life in a hundred different ways. We'll talk more about those in a later chapter.

On the other hand, depression can also be harnessed for good. Maybe you take advantage of your reduced energy to spend time reading, or maybe your experiences with depression lead you to write great poetry. Or maybe you embark on a mission to catalogue the world's saddest fences. Who knows?

TRIPPING THE LIGHT PSYCHOTIC

When I first told one of my friends I was taking antipsychotics, she smirked and said, "Oh, you're a psychopath?" Psychosis and "psychotic," its accompanying adjective, are some of the most misused mental-health words out there. First of all, antipsychotics are commonly used for reasons other than psychosis (such as sleep and mood stability), so don't be freaked out if you get prescribed an antipsychotic if you've never been psychotic. Secondly, being psychotic is a totally different thing from being a psychopath. "Psychopathy" means the tendency towards violent, antisocial behavior. Psychosis is when you have delusional beliefs and hallucinations; it can range from experiencing a completely different reality from other people and having no insight, to experiencing voices and visual hallucinations and having some insight into the fact that this experience is not being shared by people around you. Psychosis is on a continuum: some experiences are very close to "normal" reality and some are quite far away. In some cultures, what we call psychosis is associated with shamanism and celebrated as a connection with the underworld. I'm just sayin'.

HALLUCINATIONS

Hallucinations can be auditory, visual, tactile, or even olfactory. You might see people who aren't really there or hear voices giving you commands. Hallucinations can be more or less scary, and they can also be caused by lack of sleep. Like the other aspects of psychosis, hallucinations are on the spectrum of normal human experience and can range from interesting to terrifying and dangerous.

DELUSIONS

Delusions are tricky, because there is such a fine line in our society between which beliefs are considered acceptable and which are considered insane. For example, millions of people hold the same "perfectly normal" religious beliefs that would be considered bizarre and outlandish if they were held by a single person. The *DSM-V* defines a delusion as "a false belief based on incorrect inference about external reality that is firmly sustained despite what almost everybody else believes and despite what constitutes incontrovertible and obvious proof or evidence to the contrary. The belief is not one ordinarily accepted by other members of the person's culture or subculture." A good example of a delusion is the belief that you're being held captive by kidnappers, when really the "kidnappers" are your stoner roommates who wouldn't even notice if you left the house. If you're delusional, it can be hard to believe friends who tell you your delusions are false. You might believe they're lying, thereby interpreting their comments in a way that confirms your version of reality.

THOUGHT DISORDER

Thought disorder is easiest to identify in a person's speech or writing. It's characterized by a person not making sense from one sentence to the next or making associations that don't make sense to anyone else. For example: "The plane left the airport at three o'clock, and therefore the daisies in the bowl were put there by the dragon."

LACK OF INSIGHT

In psychiatry, insight means the ability to recognize when your behavior and thought patterns are coming from your mental illness as opposed to your regular self. For example: "I realize that the voices in my head aren't coming from real people, even though it really feels like they are."

Insight can vary drastically in psychotic episodes. A person experiencing a full-blown episode of psychosis may not realize that the person sitting next to them on the bus can't also see that the bus is being driven by the Hindu deity Ganesh. Another person experiencing psychosis might slip in and out of insight, alternately realizing that their reality isn't shared and believing that it is. A third person might be aware the whole time that nobody else can see what they're seeing.

Troubles with insight are not unique to people experiencing psychosis, or to people with mood disorders. Pretty much every human you can meet on this planet has a lack of insight about some aspect of his or her life: from your college roommate who just can't seem to understand why things aren't working out with Enrique (note to roommate: Enrique is a major dick! Break up with him already!) to your little brother's lack of insight as to why the other kids don't want to play with him (you need to stop wearing that werewolf mask, little bro . . .). If we all had perfect insight at all times, we'd be enlightened sages, in perfect harmony with ourselves and our world. But we don't, and so we run into problems—whether that's problems with believing Enrique will *finally* fall in love with us, or problems with believing there's a secret research lab at Stanford University devoted to harvesting our memories with the help of a highly trained team of cyborg rats.

In chapter 5, I will talk about tools for developing insight, which can help you to gain much more control over depression, mania, psychosis, and everyday life.

———◆———

Like with any other aspect of bipolar disorder, the boundaries of what we call psychosis are not firmly defined; what matters most is not how your experience is categorized by the *DSM-V,* but whether it's having a positive or destructive effect on your life. For example, a lucky person with a great amount of insight, self-discipline, and support from friends and family might be able to treat psychosis as a spiritual experience. For a person who has no support system, no insight, and a comorbidity like substance abuse, psychosis might just be a hellish experience.

OTHER ASPECTS OF BIPOLAR DISORDER

RAPID CYCLING

Rapid cycling means having four or more episodes of mania or depression within a twelve-month period. Rapid cyclers may also have more frequent changes of mood within a week, day, hour, or even minute; the ups and downs are accelerated, and therefore harder to treat. But here's the good news: rapid cycling is not a life sentence. Factors such as drug use and lifestyle can fuel the accelerated cycle of episodes, and a change in lifestyle can significantly slow down the cycles.

MIXED STATES

A mixed state is like a delicious sundae made with both caramel sauce *and* cod liver oil, served on a tantalizing waffle cone of rage. A mixed state is the term for when you experience both manic and depressive symptoms at the same time for at least a week. They generally fall into two categories: dysphoric mania and agitated depression—yin and yang. The former is mania accompanied by things like anger and thoughts of suicide, and the latter is depression with symptoms of hypomania. Not as much is known about mixed states as about vanilla mania or depression, and many people's real experiences of mixed episodes don't meet the diagnostic criteria. Like rapid cycling, this is one of those gray areas that will probably see its definition tweaked a lot over the next hundred years.

CYCLOTHYMIA

Cyclothymia, sometimes referred to as "bipolar lite," is when you have normal moods interspersed with periods of dysthymia (depression too mild to qualify as major depression) and periods of hypomanic symptoms.

"Hey, that sounds like everyone I know. Does the whole world have cyclothymia?"

Not quite. The *DSM-V* specifies that the symptoms must "cause the patient clinically significant distress or impair work, social, or personal functioning." Furthermore, the euphoric highs and depressive lows in cyclothymia are not in response to life events, but come about for no apparent reason—at least one episode every two months. Cyclothymia sometimes develops into bipolar disorder and, like bipolar disorder, appears to have a genetic component.

LAST THOUGHTS ON THIS STUFF

BIPOLAR ISN'T EVERYTHING

I told you we were going to go through the *DSM* definitions of mania, depression, and other official bipolar words because you're going to run into them anyway. Satisfied? Now, I want to remind you of something very important: human experience is a very wide and varied thing. If you categorize every intense experience in your life as being "bipolar" (and by definition, pathological, abnormal, wrong, undesirable, something to be fixed or changed), you will do yourself a grave disservice. There are plenty of experiences and states of being that are painful and disruptive in a meaningful and ultimately very positive way— and if we label them all as pathological or medicate them out of existence, we'll miss out on their gifts.

For example: a couple years ago, my meditation practice led me to a place where I became extremely sensitive to sounds. I could not only hear the engines of every passing car, but I could *feel* the sound's vibrations. The humming fridge, the buzzing lights, the hissing kettle, and the sounds of people's voices were overwhelming in their clarity and detail, to the point that I tried wearing ear plugs with heavy-duty shop headphones over them just to get some silence. I sat with my drums for hours, driven to tears by the impossibility of getting them exactly in tune, but trying and trying to do so. I couldn't sleep—my ears were so wide open, I just *heard* things all night.

Now, if I happened to be carrying a bipolar hammer, that experience would look very much like a "manic" nail. Not sleeping? Check. Seemingly erratic behavior? Check. Bring on the lithium, right? From a Western psychiatric perspective, this undeniably painful experience would be something to "treat." But from the perspective of a musician and meditation student, it was a pretty normal and expected phase. Sound was driving me crazy; and why not? Sound is crazy. Sound is amazing. If you go down the rabbit hole of sound, you make some pretty wild discoveries. And so I spent a month or two being driven completely insane by the sounds around me . . . and then the phase passed. I started sleeping again. I could sit in a room with cars passing without writhing in pain. I wasn't "recovering from an episode." Bipolar disorder didn't even cross my mind. It was clear to me, both then and now, that what happened was meaningful, necessary, useful, and to some extent, expected.

Conclusion? Mania, depression, and psychosis aren't always the appropriate lenses through which to view your experiences. Sometimes the appropriate lens is grief; sometimes it's religious or spiritual experience; sometimes it's culture; sometimes it's another context altogether. Before you go around banging nails, be aware of which hammer you're holding, and ask yourself if there are other possibilities.

THAT'S SO BIPOLAR:
CINDY SHMOE'S GUIDE TO HOW
EVERYONE IS, LIKE, SO BIPOLAR

1. OK, so my manager at Tatlow's is, like, so bipolar. One day she's totally nice to me, and the next day she's like, "Why did you dump a pitcher of beer on that guy's head?"

2. Shakespeare prof? Completely bipolar. In class, he's all really energetic and bouncy, and then when I went to pick up my brilliant essay I wrote about how Lady Macbeth is really hearing voices from Joseph Stalin, he acted all sad and depressed.

3. My boyfriend is, like, the most bipolar person I know. When we're out at the club dancing, he looks like he's having such a good time. Then suddenly he gets all mad, and he's like, "Did you just steal my credit card and buy six bottles of hundred-year-old champagne?" And I'm, like, "Obviously."

4. The crazy neighbor lady is such a sad case. I really feel bad for her. She's always coming over to our house to complain about the noise from the building projects I like to do at night. I just hope her kids find her a good rest home.

5. My parents? Bipolarest freaks in town. No, they're both, like, actually bipolar. I'm just glad I don't live with them anymore—it's probably contagious.

3

YOU'VE GOT DRUGS
WRAPPING YOUR HEAD AROUND MEDS

Imagination time!

You are hospitalized during a manic episode. After a few days of observation, your doctor says, "You seem to be suffering a mind-body malfunction, or possibly experiencing some sort of long-repressed trauma. What I'd like you to do is move to a sweet little cabin in the woods, practice tai chi, learn deep breathing exercises, make art, and eat plenty of kale. The cabin will come with a bicycle you can use to get to appointments with this really groovy therapist who will help you integrate your experience and move towards finding stability and meaningful participation in society. Don't worry about work or school—your treatment will be completely funded by the government. It's a neat little program we have for people experiencing extreme mental states, and the recovery rate is simply superb! PS. While you are at the cabin, we will also be working with your family and wider community to make sure you come home to a healthy and supportive environment."

If I could run the world, this is what would happen when people were diagnosed with bipolar, depression, or just about any kind of mental unrest. There would be nature time, meditation, relief from the pressures of industrial society, and plenty of support to help people learn better patterns of body and mind (not to mention a gentler and kinder world to come home to).

However, I don't run the world—and so a typical bipolar scenario goes more like this:

You are hospitalized during a manic episode. After a few days of observation, your doctor says, "You have bipolar disorder! I am writing you a prescription for ZypraXanaQueloRex. Come back in three weeks, but call me sooner if you find yourself chewing off your own arm while you sleep—that's a rare side effect, but it happens."

In North America in the year 2017, having bipolar disorder is often assumed to mean taking meds for life. But "meds for life" does not begin to sum up the incredibly wide range of treatment patterns available for people diagnosed with bipolar. Some people choose to take some combination of meds for the rest of their lives. Some people take medication for the first year or two following a major psychiatric event, then gradually off-ramp certain meds (or even all meds) as they stabilize their lives and learn alternative methods for managing stress and dealing with symptoms. Some people try every alternative treatment possible and use meds as a last resort. Some people would *like* to be off meds, but can't seem to get by without them; and some people never take psychiatric medication at all.

This chapter is all about those little bottles of pills with the weird names: what they can do for you and what they can't, when they're useful and when they're less useful, and how to be an effective participant in your own mental health care.

WHY MEDS?

Sometimes you can fix your problems by doing yoga, hanging out with different people, doing a ton of creative visualization, and drinking only the purest artisanal "happy" springwater—and sometimes you can't. Taking medication is different from other ways of helping yourself, because medication acts directly on your brain chemistry. Doctors prescribe medications for bipolar because meds produce fast, observable results. Manic person running around psych ward? *Bam!* Meds'll take that sucker down a notch. Depressed person sobbing on couch? *Bam!* Now they're crying in the grocery store aisle. (Meds can help a depressed person regain a little functioning.)

Psychiatric medications have been criticized for this reason: because they work so fast and so effectively, some people fear that they're being used as a replacement for fixing the root causes and behaviors that feed into a mental illness. But medications are also very practical for the same reason: you can't deal with the root causes of your illness if you're too busy being crazy. It's another yin-and-yang situation: meds help you get to a point where you can help yourself in other ways, and helping yourself in other ways can help you be less reliant on meds.

WHY TAKE PSYCH MEDS? WHAT MEDICATION CAN AND CAN'T DO

Many symptoms of bipolar disorder can be alleviated by meditation, cognitive behavioral therapy, or a good old-fashioned whiskey bender. So why take prescription drugs at all? Here is a handy chart to get you thinking about the differences and similarities:

Bipolar Symptom	Psych Meds	Whiskey Bender	Cognitive Behavioral Therapy	Meditation
Insomnia	Makes you groggy *right now.*	Makes you black out	Identify thoughts and behaviors fueling insomnia	Teaches you to relax . . . with practice.
Depression	Lifts your mood *right now.*	Numbs the pain	Identify thoughts and behaviors fueling depression	Helps you find peace . . . with practice.
Mania	Stabilizes your mood *right now.*	Blurs your mood	Identify thoughts and behaviors fueling mania	Teaches you to observe impulses without acting on them . . . with practice.
Psychosis	Stop being psychotic *right now.*	Get more psychotic . . . right now!	Identify thoughts not in line with consensus reality	Om . . . with practice.
Side Effects	Rashes, weight gain	Vomiting, nausea	Too much identifying!	Beatific smile, equanimity

As you can see, bipolar symptoms like insomnia and depression can be greatly eased by meditation or cognitive behavioral techniques, but it takes practice and dedication to work—more dedication and practice than most people are willing or able to commit, at least when their world is still in chaos from a first episode. Medication, on the other hand, starts working pretty quickly and doesn't demand a whole lot from you other than taking it at the right time. Most people in our modern industrial society simply can't afford to quit their jobs or schooling in order to devote the enormous amount of time it takes to master the skills taught by meditation or cognitive behavioral therapy, or to rearrange their lives in such a way that their bipolar symptoms aren't triggered by day-to-day stressors. And some people have such difficult and persistent symptoms that even if they could move to the proverbial cabin in the woods with nothing but a box of incense and a cognitive behavioral therapy workbook, they'd still be better off taking medication.

My point is this: psychiatric medication is one tool among many, and how and when you decide to use that tool depends on a number of factors. How extreme a state are you in? How stable is your living situation? A person who was just hospitalized for full-blow mania and a person who has only had a "taste" of hypomania will have different factors to take into consideration. No two people diagnosed with bipolar are the same; and no person diagnosed with bipolar is the same year to year and decade to decade. Decisions about medication ought to reflect this.

Here is a story about the way your relationship to psych meds can change depending on circumstances. At the time I was diagnosed with bipolar disorder, I was sleeping so little I was barely lucid. Psychiatric meds put me to sleep—a relief I desperately needed. It was too late in the game to start cognitive behavioral therapy or meditation classes; I was already too close to the edge, and just needed someone to press the Off switch. Psych meds were very effective at getting me to sleep, which helped me to get my life back on track. I was in college, and too busy with classes and friends to devote much thought to debugging my insomnia.

Over the years, I began to take a closer look at my insomnia and the anxiety and hyperactivity that fueled it. I began to practice mindfulness and deep breathing, and to question some of the false beliefs I had about sleep. Finally, *when these practices were firmly established,* I stopped taking the medication, and have had no problems with insomnia ever since (and far fewer problems with the anxiety and hypomania that were fueling it before).

At twenty, I'm not sure I could have tackled my insomnia with therapy or mind-body techniques even if it had occurred to me to try (which it did not!)—my living situation was too stressful, my support network nonexistent, and I had to finish school and couldn't afford to be nonfunctional for weeks or months while I played around with nonmedication approaches. At thirty, all of those pressures have gone away: I have a stable living situation, I set my own hours, and I have the time and space to work on myself, instead of merely struggling to get by. My relationship to medication changed because my life changed—as most lives do, slowly or quickly.

Now, boys and girls, am I saying "check out a library book about mindfulness, get really excited about the idea, and stop taking your meds that very night"? (All together now: "No, Hilary!") Am I saying "it is possible to establish practices that help you deal with sleep and mood with less medication or no medication—over as many months or years as it takes and with proper and ongoing support and guidance"? (All together now: "Yes, Hilary!")

MEDICATION: JUST ONE PIECE OF THE PIE

Some people assume that simply taking medication is an effective way of dealing with bipolar disorder, but this couldn't be further from the truth. ZypraXanaQueloRex can take down your mania and prevent future manic episodes, but it can't stop you from going on whiskey benders, it can't heal your relationship with your dad, it can't fix your nagging back pain, it can't change your beliefs about life, and it can't stop developers from draining your favorite swamp to build a shopping mall.

From this point of view, ZypraXanaQueloRex is only one piece in a pretty complex pie. Maybe tai chi is another piece; maybe talk therapy is another piece; maybe protesting the shopping mall is another piece; maybe going to Alcoholics Anonymous is another piece; maybe addressing your physical health is another piece. If you take away any of these pieces, the pie is gonna leave you hungry.

People who don't understand this concept are often frustrated or angry when their lives don't improve after taking medication: "What the hell! I'm taking ZypraXanaQueloRex, and I'm still depressed/hypomanic. I must be soooo bipolar that nothing works." The problem here is not that "nothing works"—the problem is attempting to use a single dart for a condition that doesn't have a single target. You can take a pill to make a headache go away; but you can't take a pill to solve every problem of being a human, especially a human with intense moods and energy cycles. You need to approach the situation from *all* directions, not just one. ZypraXanaQueloRex may be useful or even essential for you, but it will never do everything you desire. You've got to remember the rest of the pie.

Taking psychiatric meds for the first time can be a catalyst for thinking about the big questions in life, such as, "What is reality?" and "Who am I?" Are you still authentically *you* when you take mind-altering medication? What about when you have a mind-altering disorder? These are real questions for *everyone*, but for most people, the answers don't affect them in such a concrete way. You're lucky/unlucky enough that you *need* to grapple with these questions because they'll affect real decisions you have to make. Let's examine some beliefs about medication and how they play out with regards to these questions.

BELIEF #1: "IF I GO ON MEDS, IT MEANS I'VE FAILED."

Being put on psychiatric medication can be a very emotional experience. Often, a person has been struggling for a long time, and has tried *everything* to cure their anxiety, depression or mania—exercise, meditation, therapy, even moving to a new city or joining a new religion (maybe both! I mean, who *hasn't* run away to LA to join the Hare Krishna in the hopes that it will solve all their problems?). And after all those months or years of hard work and struggle, a doctor comes along and writes a prescription in about five seconds.

Sure, some people are relieved to finally get the pills. But it can also be crushingly disappointing. It feels like all those things you put your hopes in weren't enough, and all those people who tried to help you weren't enough either. (Your yoga teacher spent months teaching you deep breathing—what would she think if she knew you were on meds now?) Maybe if you had just *tried harder*, you could have made it another month or year without medication. Or if your friends and family would have just left you alone, you could have figured things out—if only they hadn't interrupted your progress with that humiliating "intervention."

Over the years, I have met a *lot* of people diagnosed with bipolar, many of whom were on medication. And guess what? Not a single one of them was on meds because they were lazy or bad or hadn't tried hard enough. In fact, they were some of the kindest, most hardworking, and earnest people you could ever meet. They were doing everything they could to have good lives and be present for their friends and families. And far from giving up on the exercise, meditation, and therapy that hadn't been "enough" before, they took advantage of the stability they gained with the help of meds to strengthen these practices even more.

BELIEF #2: "TAKING MEDS HAS CHANGED WHO I AM."

Grieving for a perceived former self is a normal part of dealing with a bipolar diagnosis. Before, you were healthy, normal, vivid, and emotive. Then suddenly, your wires frayed. Now you take meds every night. You feel like a different person, in part because you're not having the same moods as before and in part because the old you didn't take meds. Maybe you feel guilty for betraying the old you by subduing her with medication, and you want to let her out. Maybe you're afraid your meds are making you act differently, making you flat or boring. Sometimes they are. (Ask a friend.)

People are very bad at remembering how things really were. It's easier to observe this in, say, some old people, who pine for the good old days when everything was perfect. But it's true for you too. The good old days before you had bipolar sucked a lot too.

This yearning for the pre-bipolar self is an elusive, slippery thing. When I'm depressed, I long for my happy self. When I'm feeling old, I long for my younger self. It's human nature to think the grass was greener on the other side of the psychiatric fence. And sometimes it really is greener. When you sleep eight hours a night, you lose a certain edge. Even when they hurt, mood cycles make life interesting. Rats have been observed giving themselves electric shocks rather than suffering boredom. When medication makes your mood cycles lose their frequency and intensity, you need to find other sources of magic and foment in your life. You need to find other ways to define yourself and fill your time outside of being manic or depressed.

At the end of the day, only you can decide if being on meds and stable is worth the loss of your old self. But don't make a false god of that old self; chances are that hindsight has bumped it up a few notches from how it really was. And you can never stay the same way forever. Meds or not, you'll keep on growing and changing your whole life.

Things to Consider: What defines an "authentic" experience? Are you authentically you when you're on medication? What about when you're manic or depressed? Do certain medications allow you to feel more like yourself than others?

BELIEF #3: "I MUST BE REALLY WEIRD AND FREAKISH IF I NEED MEDS."

You need meds because you're a creepy, screwed-up freak of nature, right? Otherwise, how do all those people in the world get to sleep without Klonopin or get up in the morning without Epival?

This is a tough part of being diagnosed with a mental illness: the feeling that you're maimed or incompetent in a way that other people are not.

OK, now pay attention. Here is where wizened old Hilary is going to pull up a chair and dispense some wisdom. As mentioned a couple paragraphs ago, I have met a *lot* of people diagnosed with bipolar over the years, and from what I have observed, what distinguishes them from the general population is not freakishness or weakness, but sensitivity. I've met people with bipolar who are exquisitely attuned to nature, or have an uncanny sense of color and sound. I've met people with bipolar who are so attuned to other people's emotions they almost seem psychic, or are so good with animals that cats and dogs and dolphins literally come running or swimming up to meet them. This incredible sensitivity is a great gift and is one reason why so many people with bipolar become great artists, actors, musicians, or inventors—but it can also cause a tremendous amount of suffering. A person with an uncanny sense of sound might be a brilliant musician, but might also be overwhelmed or driven to mania by the sounds of modern reality (cars, planes, refrigerators, jackhammers). A person who is sensitive to nature might delight in the forest more than most, but might also be driven to depression or even suicidality by the destruction of the natural world.

The truth is, we don't live in an age that is particularly easy or kind to highly sensitive people. The world is noisy, crowded, fast-paced, and full of stressful demands: if you don't work your shift at Burgertown, you can't pay your rent, and if you can't pay your rent, you get evicted, and if you get evicted, you end up on the street, and if you end up on the street, you can't sleep, and if you can't sleep, you get really, really sick. Is it any surprise that so many people end up on meds, bipolar or not? It's *hard* to live in an industrial society. If you need meds to survive it, that doesn't mean you're a freak or an inferior person: you're just a person trying to get by. And that is *OK.*

PROBLEMS WITH MEDS

Some people find that medication helps them regain stability and live a relatively "normal" life. I've talked to many people who are passionate about their meds—who finally feel OK after years of struggle, or credit medication for helping them get through work or school and be present with their families instead of missing out in the psych ward. However, there are also many people who have unhappy experiences with meds, and stop taking them with or without their doctor's blessing. There are all sorts of reasons why people with bipolar disorder (and other mental illnesses) go off their meds. Here are a few of them:

THE MEDS' USEFULNESS DOESN'T JUSTIFY THEIR SIDE EFFECTS

You're taking these pills for your mood swings, but you've lost your creativity and all you do now is watch TV. Oh, and you're groggy and twenty pounds overweight. Your bipolar is "under control," but your life has lost its color, so what's the point?

IT'S TOO HARD TO MAINTAIN CONTINUITY.

You saw a doctor in Denver who prescribed lithium, and that was OK for a while. Then you moved to Boulder, and the doctor there said you didn't have bipolar at all, but General Anxiety Disorder, and put you on Ativan. When you finished school, you moved to Honolulu and the doctor there said you were just depressed and had you do a few cognitive behavioral therapy sessions, but then your insurance sent you a bill for $900 and it almost made you lose your apartment so you stopped. Lately you've been doing something called Chakra Therapy with this lady you met at the food co-op–she only charges $20 an hour, and even though you know it's kinda cheesy, the truth is she actually helps you understand your problems, unlike any of the doctors you've seen.

THE MEDS DON'T GET AT THE ROOT OF YOUR PROBLEMS.

You haven't had a manic episode since going on lithium—but none of the doctors seem equipped to deal with the fact that you grew up in an abusive household, that you were traumatized in the army, that you suffer from constant back pain, and that you've been semi-homeless for the past six months. They genuinely want to help, but it seems like your problems are just too big for anyone to handle, and eventually you just drop out.

THE MEDS STOPPED WORKING.

You were on QueloPraxoLine for three years and were pretty happy with it, but shortly after your twenty-fifth birthday your symptoms started creeping back, and now you're barely sleeping again. What's the point of taking the meds if they aren't even going to work?

YOU ARE BEING OVERMEDICATED.

Your doctor wants to keep you on 1200 mg of Whack-AMoleARyl "just to be safe" even though you haven't had a manic episode in ten years. It all seems a little over-the-top, especially since the WhackAMole makes you feel like your brain is stuffed with cotton balls. Do you really need to spend the rest of your life at that level of sedation just because you were manic one time when you were twenty-two?

YOU ARE IN THE MIDST OF A MANIC OR PSYCHOTIC EPISODE AND HAVE LOST INSIGHT.

Why should you take meds? You are the Archangel Michael, and the Archangel Michael doesn't take meds.

WhackAMoleARyl impedes your ability to see people's brainwaves, and that ability is going to be crucial if you are going to win the battle against the Dark Forces . . .

YOU HAVE FOUND SOMETHING THAT WORKS BETTER THAN MEDS, AND THEY ARE NO LONGER NECESSARY.

Sure, meds seemed pretty crucial when you were twenty-five and living in your van with your boyfriend, the coke dealer—but you've figured out a lot of stuff since then, and you're just a more stable person generally. You exercise, volunteer, get good sleep, eat right, stopped drinking and doing drugs. You're pretty sure that what they called a hypomanic episode was just normal twenty-something stuff—you've been fine without meds for five years now.

———◆———

These problems with meds are all extremely common, to the point where it would be hard to find a person diagnosed with bipolar disorder who has not struggled with one or more of them. Some of these problems can be mitigated by better communication with one's doctor, but some of them stick around in some form regardless of what you do: the truth is, meds *do* have side effects, they *do* sometimes stop working, and they are *not* a complete solution to life's suffering. They can also interfere with experiences that may be important or meaningful to you (such as seeing brainwaves!) even though they don't seem important to anyone else.

The negative reasons people go off meds tend to hog most of the attention, but people also go off meds for *positive* reasons, such as when they've made such drastic improvements in their health, lifestyle, and coping strategies they no longer need them. For example, a person who has done a lot of work on debugging mood cycles and developing insight may decide to taper off meds—and this decision should be supported and assisted, rather than condemned.

Here are some actions to take when you're having problems with medication or you're considering going off meds entirely:

FIGURE OUT WHAT THE *REAL* PROBLEM IS.

Is the problem really that you don't want to be on meds at all? Or is it that you're having trouble with these particular meds, or that your dose is too high, or that you don't like your doctor and therefore don't want to do anything he/she says? Maybe you really do want to go 100 percent med-free—but maybe, when you really think about it, you're frustrated about something else. You can't tackle your problem until you correctly identify what your problem is. It's worth spending some time poking around in your mind and emotions to make sure you're targeting the right culprit, and not a decoy. A friend, teacher, or trusted family member or therapist could help you have this conversation, if you're having trouble figuring it out on your own.

GET A SECOND (OR THIRD) OPINION.

Doctors aren't gods. If you've been seeing Dr. X for a long time, you might start to believe that taking 1200 mg of WhackAMoleARyl is your only option, even though it makes your brain fog and your legs go numb—but if you went and talked to Dr. Y, she might be perfectly happy to have you try a lower dose and see how it goes, or she might recommend a newer drug that doesn't have WhackAMoleARyl's side effects. (It turns out Dr. X has been prescribing 1200 mg of WhackAMoleARyl since he graduated from med school in 1969, and hasn't bothered to update his knowledge or prescribing practices since then. Uh, maybe you shouldn't go to that doctor anymore. . . .)

CONSULT AN ASTROLOGER.

Just checking to see if you were paying attention! What I really mean is: take a realistic inventory of your situation, and ask yourself if the conditions of your life support you going off meds at this time. Is Mercury in retrograde? Is Mars in the seventh . . . I mean, are you in a stable living situation? Do you have good insight into your moods, and have you developed good ways of recognizing the early warning signs of mania and depression and curbing them before they get out of hand? Do you have a ton of stressful responsibilities right now (like finishing your master's thesis or getting ready for a new baby) or are the next few months of your life pretty clear and open?

Speaking from experience: trying to taper off meds when you are homeless, on a big work or school deadline, or when you haven't *truly* developed the skills necessary to survive without them is going to be an exercise in unnecessary suffering. It's a little like planning a successful vegetable garden: if you plant out your tomato starts too early, you're going to be disappointed when they get nuked by an unexpected frost. If you wait until the time is *really* right, you have a much better chance of having them survive and thrive.

This point is so important I am going to repeat it, in bold: **Simply quitting medication is usually not the best plan. You need to learn skills to replace the function the medication provided.** Otherwise, you'll end up with your same old symptoms, which is why you were put on meds in the first place. I will talk more about ways of developing these skills in a later chapter.

IT'S ALL YOU

If you're a miserable jerk, going on psychiatric meds will alleviate your bipolar symptoms, but it won't make you *stop* being a miserable jerk. If you were a happy person before coming down with bipolar, you should still be a happy person on meds. If you were a bitchy, cranky person before being diagnosed bipolar, you'll still be a huge bitch on meds. Medication affects the parts of yourself you can't easily control, like your brain chemistry. Medication will not take care of the things you *can* control, like your worldview, your habits, and your reactions to life events.

Happy people are happy because out of the huge gamut of possible reactions to any given event or situation, they consistently choose the positive ones. If a happy person is starving, her face will shine with anticipation of the next delicious meal. A miserable person, however, will have an inner dialogue focusing on how starving and miserable she is. If a happy person gets diagnosed bipolar, she might be worried about it for a while, but ultimately carry on with a normal, exuberant life. If a miserable person gets bipolar, no amount of medication will make her feel less miserable—less manic, yes, but not less miserable.

Solution? Be aware at all times of the many responses you could have to any situation. As much as you can, choose patience over impatience, calm over frustration, grace over fear, and happiness over disappointment. The decisions you make from moment to moment are more powerful than any medication in determining your overall happiness in life.

ACTUALLY, IT'S NOT ALL YOU

In North America, the thing we call mental illness is usually talked about as something that happens to you or perhaps inside you. This has led to a massive shifting of responsibility away from society and onto the individual: "it's *your* responsibility to fix *yourself* because *you're* the one with a problem."

When you stop to examine this philosophy, it makes absolutely no sense. Everything in this world is connected to everything else; if there is illness at one level, chances are there's illness at another level. Think about the pine beetle epidemic that has ravaged forests in the West. You could point a finger at any given beetle-infested tree in British Columbia or Colorado and say, "That pine is sick! That pine has a problem!" And yet you could just as truthfully point your finger at the poor forest management practices and climate change factors that made the trees vulnerable to the beetles in the first place. Are the trees sick, is the system sick, or are they just different manifestations of one underlying reality?

The same is true of mental illnesses. Like the pine trees, we are all under pretty serious stress: stress from noise, from pollution and overcrowding, from a million different factors. Sure, you can say that a person with bipolar is ill—but so is the stressful system that perpetuates the conditions in which the illness can flourish. I like to think that as we mend the world—by restoring natural areas, improving food systems, and developing healthier relationships—the incidence rate of mental illness and anxiety will decline accordingly.

So even if you do take medication to help with your mood and mental state, don't discount the social, political, economic, historical, and environmental forces at play in creating your mental distress. Work to make the world a better place for all people and all creatures. After all, it's not all about you.

4

SHRINKS
WHAT THEY'RE FOR AND HOW THEY CAN HELP

WHY SHRINKS?

In medieval Wales there were poor men and women known as sin-eaters, whose job it was to eat the sins of folks who'd died so the dead person's soul could go to heaven. Their job sucked. The family of the deceased person would pass the sin-eater bread and wine over the coffin to symbolize the transfer of sins from the dead person to the sin-eater. Then the dead person would waltz into heaven, his family would be relieved, and the sin-eater would get a piece of bread and a pile of damnation.

Shrinks are sin-eaters, minus the poverty, coffins, and eternal damnation. They specialize in receiving all your psychic ills—all the dredged-up memories, patterns, abuses, delusions, and baggage you carry around. It's a shrink's job to listen to your stories and ask for more. Because you're paying them top dollar to listen, there's no guilt in talking about yourself for an hour. Unlike unburdening to a best friend, you don't have to worry about your shrink's needs or make sure she's getting enough support from the relationship. She's your sin-eater; your pain is her gain. Because your psychiatrist isn't part of your family or social group, you don't have to worry that anything you say will screw up your relationships or damage anyone's trust in you. She has nothing to lose or gain from anything you say or do, and is, therefore, objective. The client-shrink relationship is, by definition, unbalanced. Or rather, it's balanced by cash—piles of cold, hard cash. You show up and give your shrink an honest account of your mind, and she listens, guides you to understanding, and prescribes pills to help you out in the afterlife.

Psychiatrists exist to step in when the general population is no longer qualified to deal with your shit. You go to a shrink when:

- *You're manifesting symptoms and behaviors that most non-shrinks can't identify or make sense of.*

  Psychiatrists have seen people like you in patterns like yours hundreds of times. They understand what the "bipolar" pattern looks like and can even predict how it will unfold in the future. Whereas your best friend might love you, but not understand the difference between mania and a caffeine buzz, your shrink doesn't love you (ouch, I said it!), but knows her diagnostic ass from her elbow. She also has studied and, perhaps more important, *seen* the difference between bipolar, drug addiction, schizophrenia, alcoholism, and hypochondriacs who love to be diagnosed.

- *You need an objective outsider to talk to.*

  Your struggle with a mental illness can put a lot of stress on your relationships with your family and friends. Even a close friend can only handle so much without feeling drained. On the other hand, you can work through all your toxic baggage with a shrink with no fear of straining or damaging your intimate relationships. Talking to a shrink is cathartic precisely because the shrink is not involved in your life in other ways. Your friends don't even have to know you're seeing one.

- *You need someone to prescribe and monitor your meds.*

  Psychiatrists are allowed to prescribe meds and tweak them according to your needs. Of course, you don't have to see a psychiatrist every week for as long as you're on psychiatric meds, but if you're still trying to find a combination of drugs that works for you, or if your existing meds suddenly stop working, a psychiatrist will help you get your feet back on solid ground. A psychiatrist can also help you wean off medication safely if that's a choice you want to make.

The following table highlights the differences between three popular therapeutic options:

	Best Friend	Psychiatrist	Hell's Angels
Experienced with insanity?	Read *Touched With Fire.*	Went to med school, has seen a lot of different people.	Yes.
Prescribes drugs?	Can't.	Can.	Lots.
Talk about your problems?	Yes.	Yes.	Favors chain beatings.
Is objective?	Dates your brother.	Doesn't.	Whacked your brother.

FUNCTIONS OF A SHRINK

Now that we've talked about why you might see a shrink, let's take a closer look at the specific functions of a shrink.

Outside of abstract notions like healing and catharsis, what are the practical, concrete functions of a psychiatrist or therapist? Which of those functions are unique to licensed therapists/psychiatrists, and which can be filled by free resources like friends, support groups, and books?

Going to a shrink lets you:

- check in with someone.
- talk about yourself and about private, sensitive issues.
- get advice and prescriptions (from psychiatrists only, not psychologists) for your medications.
- see someone who can connect you to other mental-health resources.
- do something productive that gives you a sense of positive action over your disorder.

Seeing a shrink can also:

- help you gain traction in your life.
- help you understand your diagnosis.
- help you identify maladaptive (counterproductive, negative) thoughts and behaviors and replace them with useful ones.
- act as sounding board for whether certain thoughts or behaviors are irrational.
- help you plan for the future, set goals, and decide on actions to take.
- give you the opportunity to talk about relationships and family stuff with someone who's uninvolved.
- give you a regular, scheduled activity.

Obviously, seeing a psychiatrist isn't the only way to get a regular, scheduled activity into your life or feel like you're being proactive about bipolar. You could just as easily join a bowling league or attend a support group. Have a look at the following table.

Functions of a Psychiatrist	Shrink	Books	Support Group	Free Clinic	Grandma
Listen to your problems	X		X	X	X
Help you understand your diagnosis	X	X	X	X	
Act as a sounding board	X		X	X	X
Help you plan and set goals	X	X		Maybe	X
Help you identify maladaptive behaviors	X	X	Maybe	Maybe	Maybe
Provide you with a regularly scheduled activity	X		X	X	X
Tweak your medication	X				
Give medical advice	X				
Check in with you	X		X	X	X
Be an objective, uninvolved listener	X				

Think about what you want to get out of therapy. Maybe you need short-term help dealing with the emotions that a bipolar diagnosis stirred up. Maybe you're rapid cycling and need to see a psychiatrist long term as you flip through episode after episode and try out different meds. Maybe you're just thinking therapy's sexy and like the idea of having a primal-scream therapist on your roster. Whatever your reason for seeing a shrink, remember that therapy isn't a magic spell or an escape from the world; it's one of many tools you can choose to use (or not) to help you establish a better life with bipolar.

WHAT'S THE DIFFERENCE BETWEEN A PSYCHIATRIST, A PSYCHOLOGIST, A THERAPIST, AND A COUNSELOR?

Psychiatrists are physicians with medical degrees (they have "M.D." after their name). Psychologists (who come in many flavors, which we'll discuss later) have doctorates and training in psychotherapy, but do not have medical degrees. Psychiatrists are doctors of medicine, and clinical psychologists are doctors (in the academic sense) of psychology. A counselor is, generally speaking, a person with a master's in counseling, and a therapist may or may not have an advanced degree or licensure, depending on your state.

In most states, only psychiatrists are allowed to prescribe medication. This might be changing: in Louisiana and New Mexico, psychologists are now allowed to prescribe meds for mental illnesses, and Oregon recently passed a bill allowing psychologists to prescribe psychotropic drugs only. Whether or not psychologists should be allowed to prescribe drugs is an ongoing debate in the health-care community, with proponents pointing to the fact that it's more efficient for patients to see one shrink who is empowered to prescribe drugs rather than bouncing around between two different shrinks, one of whom can prescribe drugs and one of whom can't. Opponents claim that without med school training in biochemistry, pharmacology, and physiology, psychologists can't safely prescribe powerful psychotropic drugs.

Anyway, point is, many people with bipolar disorder see both a psychiatrist *and* a clinical psychologist or another kind of therapist. Talk about double-fisting!

SEND IN THE CLOWNS: THERAPY OPTIONS

Now let's have a look at a handful of different therapy options and their pros and cons. Send in the clowns!

CLOWN #1: PSYCHIATRIST

A typical session with a psychiatrist is about an hour long. Like your family doctor, she'll start off the first session by asking about your family history, medical/psychiatric history, current life circumstances, and the events that precipitated your coming in to see her. Then she'll move into psychiatrist territory, asking questions about your moods, energy levels, how much sleep you're getting, what your day-to-day life is like, and your relationships with your family, friends, and/or partner. She'll also want to know about your past: Did you have a happy childhood? Did you enjoy high school? How old were you when you started drinking, having sex, doing drugs, etc.? The psychiatrist wants to figure out certain things about you: how you deal with stress, how you view yourself in the world, how you relate to other people, and how you relate to important events in your past. If there are any specific issues going on in your life, this is the time and place to talk about them in as much depth as you need.

A good psychiatrist will also help you understand your diagnosis and help you develop strategies for avoiding future episodes. If you keep seeing a psychiatrist over an extended period of time, she'll probably get the chance to observe you in a number of different states: from really depressed to baseline to kinda speedy. Your psychiatrist is also in charge of prescribing medication and monitoring its effects on you (to the extent that she has the opportunity to observe you) and is the person to talk to about making any tweaks to your med regimen.

Good for you if: you need someone to prescribe psychiatric meds, you have life events (such as childhood abuse) you want to talk about, you want someone to check in with on a regular basis, you have a lot of questions about bipolar disorder and medication.

Not the ideal fit if: you hate the idea of talking about yourself for an hour, you feel like you have "nothing to talk about," you see traditional psychiatry as "the Man."

CLOWN #2: COGNITIVE BEHAVIORAL THERAPIST

A cognitive behavioral therapist has an advanced degree in either psychology or social work, and may also be certified by the National Association of Cognitive Behavioral Therapists (NACBT). Cognitive-behavioral therapy (CBT) is the most concrete, action-based of the mainstream psychotherapies. The therapist helps you identify which thoughts and behaviors are bringing you down, and gives you specific tasks to do to fix them. The purpose of CBT is to help you become your own therapist. Therefore, you usually plan to see a cognitive-behavioral therapist twelve to eighteen times, not indefinitely, because after a number of sessions you've hopefully developed enough skill to help yourself without regular visits to the therapist. The heart and soul of CBT is helping you identify thought patterns, behaviors, and assumptions you hold that may be reinforcing your difficulties. For example, if you deal with stress by getting angry at other people, the therapist will help you develop a new, healthier thought pattern. CBT tends to be heavy on homework. Between sessions, you'll probably have to keep a journal of stressful situations and your reactions to them, and your therapist will also give you a weekly task or experiment to complete. Pure CBT is not so much about mulling over your past and gaining insight into your subconscious as it is about taking practical, immediate action to challenge your maladaptive (read: counterproductive) behaviors. During a CBT session, you'll review your homework, set new homework, and maybe do some role playing or visualization to practice your new responses to stressful situations.

Good for you if: you want to address a specific problem (e.g., shyness, self-injury, low self-esteem, troubled relationships), you're looking for self-empowerment, and you respond well to goal-setting activities.

Not the ideal fit if: you don't have a specific issue to work on, you just need someone to talk to, you don't want to do homework between therapy sessions.

CLOWN #3: INTERPERSONAL AND SOCIAL RHYTHM THERAPIST

This clown is another kind of psychologist, with an advanced degree in psychology or social work. Interpersonal and Social Rhythm Therapy, or ISRT, targets your circadian and social rhythms in order to stabilize your bipolar disorder. An ISR therapist takes a look at everything you do in a typical day and when you do it: what time you wake up, what times you eat, what times you engage in social interaction, what time you work, what time you exercise, etc. The purpose is to help you establish the best possible rhythm of life. Interestingly, ISRT is one of the only therapies shown to be effective in treating bipolar disorder specifically. Since a big part of bipolar disorder is having your rhythm of life disrupted—for example, by insomnia, hyperactivity, and elevated or reduced desire for social interaction—ISRT researchers have found that tweaking and stabilizing your patterns of social interaction can have a real stabilizing effect on your mood. During a typical ISRT session, you'll look over the records of activity you made that week and your resulting moods. For example, you might determine that you should be getting up earlier and exercising in the morning rather than at night, or that you feel happiest when you make your first social contact of the day no later than 1 p.m. As ISRT is a relatively recent (and promising!) development in psychiatry, it might be hard to find a counseling center in your area.

Good for you if: you're a nerdy, practical type who's up on your game and interested in cutting-edge bipolar research, you could benefit from a therapeutically approved schedule, you want a way to prevent future episodes.

Not the ideal fit if: you're never going to follow the improved rhythm you and your therapist come up with, you hate schedules and are married to having an erratic lifestyle, you want insight and healing to traumatic events, not lifestyle solutions.

CLOWN #4: PSYCHOANALYST

A psychoanalyst may or may not have an advanced degree in psychology or social work (or indeed, any kind of degree. More on that later). The most glamorous of the therapies, psychoanalysis is also the most spooky. The psychoanalyst's job is to help you uncover your unconscious motivations. That's where the stereotype of "I can't figure out how to work the mail machine because Daddy never loved me" comes from. During a typical psychoanalysis session, you might talk about your dreams, play a free-association game, and discuss your relationship to the psychoanalyst herself. One of the main ideas of psychoanalysis is that your relationship to your analyst mirrors your relationship to other important people in your life. So if you feel fearful and angry towards your analyst, it might indicate fear and anger towards, say, your father. Psychoanalysis also emphasizes understanding how events in your past are getting played out in the present, and helping you move beyond traumatic experiences.

Warning: The term "psychoanalyst" is not regulated by the federal government or by most states. That means anyone can legally call herself a psychoanalyst (even me. That will be $150 an hour, please!). Look for a psychoanalyst who has been certified by the American Psychoanalytic Association—they receive rigorous clinical training and have either medical degrees or advanced degrees in psychology or social work.

Good for you if: you're interested in the subconscious, you have important relationships you need to work out, you're into Freud, you've done your research.

Not the ideal fit if: you think Freud's theories are bogus, you hate analyzing things, you want a more scientific kind of therapy approved by modern medicine.

MEDITATOR CLOWN: MINDFULNESS-BASED COGNITIVE THERAPIST

MBCT is a lesser-known (although highly promising!) form of therapy in which participants learn to observe their thoughts, feelings, and physical sensations without reacting to them. The goal is to help you recognize when you are sliding into the automatic thought processes that fuel mania and depression, and to learn to see these automatic thoughts and impulses as passing mental phenomena rather than things which are "true" or which must be acted upon. For example, you might learn to recognize when you're having a manic impulse ("I must rearrange the furniture! I just *have to* rearrange *ALL* the furniture *RIGHT NOW!*"), accept that it is there ("OK, I see my brain is telling me to rearrange all the furniture"), and simply observe it while breathing calmly instead of acting on it right away ("What do you mean don't act on it? I really need to rearrange the—oh, now my brain is thinking about rabbits. I like rabbits!")

MBCT is similar to Cognitive Behavioral Therapy in that your therapist will probably give you homework, usually in the form of simple mindfulness exercises designed to help you get some space and perspective around automatic thoughts and bringing more awareness to your breath. Where MBCT and CBT differ is that whereas Cognitive Behavioral Therapy teaches you to question the content of your thoughts ("Am I *really* a failure if I don't sell 500,000 copies of my book this year?"), Mindfulness Based Cognitive Therapy teaches you not to engage with the content of your thoughts at all, but simply observe them arising and passing away. ("Ah, I see that my brain is telling me I will be a failure if I don't sell 500,000 copies of my book. Hello thought; goodbye, thought.")

MALL CLOWN: LIFE COACH

Life coaches are not medical professionals and don't necessarily have degrees in psychology, but I include them here because some family doctors recommend life coaching to their patients and because they're a cheaper option than psychiatrists if all you need is help getting organized and determining your goals.

Life coaches come in many flavors. Some specialize in career coaching, some in life skills like how to go grocery shopping, and some will even help you become a dream date. A life coach's job is to help you clarify your needs and to set and achieve clear goals in any number of areas (relationship, job, school, personal). If you're confused about where you're going in life or what you should be doing, a good life coach will know just the right questions to ask to get you to that a-ha! moment when you realize your purpose in life (or your purpose this week). Like cognitive-behavioral therapy, life coaching is very action oriented: you will leave the session each week with a set of tasks to carry out that will get you closer to your goals. Sometimes, life coaches are recommended to people who just don't know how to get started on a particular task, like applying for college.

Life coaches are not professionally licensed, like therapists or psychiatrists. In fact, life coaching is a completely unregulated field. That means *anyone* can legally call themselves a life coach with absolutely no training, certification, or supervision. They can't prescribe medication, give psychiatric advice, or deal with things like psychosis. While awesome, sincere, committed life coaches do exist, there are plenty of unqualified "life coaches" out there who will take your money and send you home with a photocopied list of canned "affirmations" to stick on your fridge, leaving you no better equipped to deal with your life.

Good for you if: you need someone to help you get your life on track in a basic way, you need help identifying your goals and making a strategy to achieve them, you want someone who's "on your team" to act as a sounding board, you're basically stable and don't need the psychiatric services of a therapist.

Not the best fit if: you need someone who can give psychiatric counseling and medical advice (a life coach is *not* a therapist), you want to discuss your past and relationships, you need something more than help with life goals.

WISE CLOWN: MENTOR, TEACHER, ELDER

Sometimes, you are lucky enough to find a person with *no* fancy certifications or degrees who is nevertheless enormously skilled in helping people through crises and extreme states. Maybe your carpentry teacher is kinda like Yoda; her advice seems as solid as her joinery work. Or you realize your cousin Bob who did a ton of acid is the only person you can actually *talk* to. Or your neighbor is a dedicated meditator who will spend hours speaking with you about far-out subjects nobody else will touch.

Such people exist, and finding one is a great blessing. They can't solve all your problems or make your decisions for you, but they can offer a kind of perspective and presence that "certified" doctors almost never do. If you are lucky enough to encounter such a person, be grateful, and learn all you can from them. Maybe someday, you'll be able to pass on the favor to another person in need.

KID'S BIRTHDAY PARTY CLOWNS: ALTERNATIVE THERAPISTS

In addition to the five well-known flavors of mind-helpers described above, you might also hear of alternatives like somatic therapy, art therapy, music therapy, and play therapy. These therapists use activities like drumming, painting, guided visualizations, body awareness, and acting out your dreams with toys to help you gain insight and heal your psychic wounds. Alternative therapists are sometimes less expensive to see than psychiatrists, or they might charge on a sliding scale.

The measure of these alternative therapies, like the measure of the mainstream ones, is whether or not they work. Ask yourself: Does this therapy leave me better equipped to deal with my life? Does this therapy help me gain insight into my thoughts, behaviors, and disorder? Is this therapy helping me move forward? If the answer is "yes," then it doesn't matter whether the therapy is mainstream or "alternative"—it's working for you!

When any kind of therapy ceases to do the above things, you're finished. When you go into a therapy session and have absolutely nothing left to say, you're finished. When you feel like a totally stable, cool person on good terms with being bipolar, you're finished. If something comes up down the road, you can always go back.

"WHAT IF I WANT THERAPY BUT CAN'T AFFORD IT?"

Thanks to mental-health parity laws passed in 2008, health insurance companies in the United States are required to cover mental-health services at the same level as physical services. By law, health insurers can't charge higher copays for mental-health services than for "regular" doctor visits, and generally can't place limits on the number of mental-health visits allowed in a given year.

Although these are clearly positive changes, they haven't made accessing mental-health services easy or affordable for everyone. Sure, if you're lucky enough to have the Ultra Primo Super Gold Plan, you can go to a therapist every week, no copay, no problem. But if you're like most people, your health plan has a copay for therapy, which could be anywhere from $20 to $60 dollars; or you have to pay everything out of pocket until you meet your $5000 deductible; or you call every therapist on the provider list, and find that they are all dead or have moved to Florida or have a two-year waiting list or basically seem sketchy.

There's no doubt about it: clowns don't come cheap, even if you have some form of health insurance. And it can be hard to believe that a clown who charges $200 per hour to talk to suffering people is a clown you even want to talk to (at least, that's how I felt after visiting the website of one too many Zen-mindful-I'm-so-enlightened therapists when researching this book, who, PS, charge more for one session than most people pay for groceries in a week).

So what's a person who's broke and bipolar to do?

If you can't afford therapy, don't despair, for the following reasons:

- Therapy alone isn't effective at treating bipolar disorder. Tons of people (myself included) get along just fine without it. But if you really need it, and you can't get it, proceed to the next option.
- Many cities have free counseling centers or clinics that offer sliding-scale payment options. Some free clinics have "real" therapists, and some have trained volunteer counselors. Obviously, volunteer counselors are unable to give medical advice or prescribe medication, but they can fulfill the therapist's function of checking in with you, giving feedback, and providing you with a safe space to talk about your issues. Free clinics and alternative counseling centers

can be a bit of a grab bag in terms of quality, but if you think about the *function* of therapy, rather than the form it takes, you can see how a combination of free resources can add up to the value of for-payment therapy. By the way, support groups fall into the category of free resources that are "like therapy." If you're a college student, your college or university might also have a free psychiatrist on call during certain hours.

- There are tons of books available that contain much of the same information and strategies that therapists deliver. For example, you can read a Mindfulness Based Cognitive Therapy manual yourself, and practice the techniques on your own. You can order a Cognitive Behavioral Therapy workbook for depression or anxiety, and work though it alone or with a friend. If you can read, you can educate yourself about bipolar disorder, anxiety, depression, and other aspects of mental health (for that matter, you can read about meditation, Zen, nutrition, altered states of consciousness, gardening, and a million other relevant topics)—you don't need to pay a therapist to deliver this information to you.

CONCLUSION

Psychiatrists, therapists, and other health practitioners can help you make sense of your experience, find stability and meaning in your present life, and help you lay a good groundwork for future health and happiness—but they can't do the work for you. You are most likely to benefit from psychotherapy if you are open, engaged, and willing to make changes. If you are closed off ("there's nothing wrong with me! I feel no pain!") or unwilling to try new things (like keeping a journal of your moods and what triggered them), it's going to be an uphill battle. If, however, you go into the process with curiosity, patience,

and a deep well of self-compassion, you will achieve
extraordinary things. There is pretty much no limit to
how much you can learn if you are willing to observe
yourself closely and honestly—and if you can find someone you trust to help you through this process, all the
better.

5

CHANGING CHANNELS
PREVENTING EPISODES WITH INSIGHT

Think about the last time you got *really* depressed or manic. Were you just chilling, feeling totally normal, maybe playing chess with your Grandpa, when *bam*, lightning struck and the guys in white coats were hustling you into the psych ward? Or was there a progression you could only see in retrospect—you started multitasking, then you just *had* to do some shopping, then your thoughts were racing, then you got more and more enraged, and you had to drink some whiskey to calm down, and then you thought you were playing chess with your Grandpa but really your Grandpa lives in Cuba and you were playing chess with *yourself,* except *yourself* was, like, an avatar from the future?

Manic, hypomanic, and depressive episodes don't just drop out of the sky, even though it can feel that way sometimes. There are almost always warning signs and subtle cues: changes in how your body feels, changes in your thoughts and emotions, changes in what seems important or unimportant to you, changes in how you respond to people around you. Being aware of these changes is called insight, and developing insight is pretty much the *best* thing you can do to prevent future bipolar episodes.

"WHAT DO YOU MEAN, DEVELOP INSIGHT? I KNOW EVERYTHING ALREADY."

At the time I was diagnosed with bipolar disorder, I wasn't very tuned in to my own mind or body. I made it a point of pride to never give in to my body's cues, to the extent that my college boyfriend once remarked, "You're never hungry, you're never thirsty, and you're never tired." Just as I prided myself on having no apparent physical needs, I did a great job of suppressing my emotional needs. I was "never" stressed, "never" lonely, "never" upset. When I developed crippling insomnia and depression in my junior year of college, I was relieved and grateful when the doctor gave me medication, but I would have been *really* lucky if she'd questioned me about the way I managed stress. The medication was fine as an emergency measure, but it didn't help me understand myself or recognize the patterns that caused me to redline. Over the years, I kept redlining again and again, relying on medication to "shut me down" when my mind and body got wound up too tight—after all, nobody had bothered to teach me otherwise.

As I grew older, I became more and more dissatisfied with this state of affairs. Maybe there was something to my old boyfriend's observation that I was "never" tired or hungry, or my current partner's (highly irritating!)

habit of calling out when I seemed stressed but wasn't acknowledging it. Maybe there was something to all that yoga-speak about "listening to your body," stuff I'd always dismissed as new age nonsense. Maybe if I paid attention to my body, my beliefs, and my mental habits, I'd figure some stuff out. Maybe I could stop redlining.

Developing insight is a surprisingly emotional task, especially if there are aspects of your experience of which you'd rather *not* be aware. Pain, stress, fear, and anxiety are uncomfortable things to feel—there's a *reason* we try to deny their existence, or escape them through drugs, alcohol, food, or work. But there is also a paradox in play: the more aware you can become of your own stress levels, the less likely you are to drive them to a point of no return. In my case, remaining unaware of my own stress and anxiety left my body with no other option but to freak out and refuse to sleep. Once I became more aware of what was going on in my emotional and physical worlds, my body didn't need to resort to the extreme measure of insomnia anymore. And once I became more aware of my thoughts and beliefs, I stopped driving myself into hypomania.

WHAT IS INSIGHT
AND HOW CAN IT HELP WITH BIPOLAR DISORDER?

Insight means the ability to perceive yourself clearly. At a basic level, it can be as simple as knowing whether you are hungry or thirsty. At a more advanced level, it can be recognizing when certain people or situations make you anxious. At an even more advanced level, it can mean recognizing when your brain is generating thoughts that aren't necessarily true, or fears that have no basis in reality. At an even *more* advanced level, it might mean recognizing that all of reality is nothing more than a field of infinitely vibrating atoms, and the mind and body you've been working so hard to understand don't actually exist. (Don't ask me; I'm not there yet.)

Bipolar disorder is not something that can be isolated in a test tube (doctors even have a hard time differentiating it from other conditions *outside* a test tube). You can't treat bipolar without affecting other parts of your body and mind, because bipolar can't be isolated; and you can't change your relationship with your body and mind without affecting the part of you called "bipolar." Therefore, any practice that helps you become more aware, more insightful, and more calm is by definition going to help you in recognizing bipolar symptoms early or avoiding the situations that trigger them in the first place.

OBSERVE, OBSERVE, OBSERVE

A great place to start in developing insight is to take inventory of what you know about yourself: your body, your thought patterns, and your interactions with other people. But the deal with making this inventory is that you actually have to observe yourself, the way you'd observe a rare leopard in the jungle. Don't assume you know everything there is to know about the leopard's behavior. Study it. Watch closely. Does it *really* sleep in caves like you always thought, or does it spend the night in a high tree branch? Is it a solitary creature like the books say, or does it have some leopard friends it likes to spend time with? How can you tell when a leopard is sick, tired, hungry, or injured?

Don't be afraid to cast away old assumptions or to make note of less-savory details of leopard behavior (did you know leopards *smoke?*). A wishful or dishonest representation of leopard behavior isn't going to benefit anyone. The whole point is to see things as they actually are—because seeing things as they *aren't* is generally a big reason people suffer.

Full disclosure: If you had asked me to do this when I was first diagnosed with bipolar, my inventory would have been a little bit suspicious. "My name is Hilary. I am never tired, never hungry, never in physical or emotional pain, and never stressed. My relationships with other people are all totally fine. In fact, I am totally fine, except for this insomnia/depression/mania/social anxiety which is 100 percent biochemical in nature and has nothing to do with anything else I just said." Since then, I have learned quite a lot about myself, some of which I will share here as an example.

THE BODY: MIRACULOUS FOUNTAIN OF INSIGHT

Your body and how you treat it can play a big role in your moods—but you need to pay attention to hear what it's saying. Here are some questions to get you started in observing your body:

QUESTIONS TO ASK YOURSELF ABOUT YOUR BODY:

- What happens to your body when you are anxious? Do you feel more pain or less pain? Is your breathing shallow or deep, fast or slow? Does the nature of your movements change? Does your posture change?

- What happens to your body when you are depressed? Do you feel more pain or less pain? Is your breathing shallow or deep, fast or slow? Does the nature of your movements change? Do you feel hot or cold? Does your posture change? Do you walk or move differently?

- How does food affect your mood? Are you happier when you are full, empty, or somewhere in between? What happens when you go too long without eating, or when you eat too much?

- Does your body give any warning signs when you are getting stressed, overwhelmed, or agitated? Do your muscles tighten? Does your voice change? Do you start biting your nails or experiencing other physical tics?

- How does your body respond to various environments? How do you feel in a house versus in a car versus in a shopping mall versus in a forest? Which environment feels the most soothing to you? Which one is the most stressful?

- Are there any elements of the physical environment that stress you out? How does your body respond to bright lights, loud noises, crowds of people? Does this change depending on your mood?

- Are there any physical activities that make you feel less stressed, anxious, depressed, or agitated? How do you respond to a slow walk, a fast bike ride, a hot shower, a long hug? Does your mood change when you stand a different way, put on different clothing, or seek out a more or less stimulating environment?

Here are some things I know about my physical self and how it relates to my moods:

Hilary at time of bipolar diagnosis:

- Ummmm . . . I have a body. I don't pay much attention to it, except to occasionally feed it some oatmeal and take it on runs.

Current Hilary:

- When I feel particularly energetic (or, *fine,* what the people in white coats call hypomanic), my breathing gets shallow, I move around a lot, and I have a sense of extreme physical agitation. I get the feeling that I *need* to act on every physical impulse: go to the hardware store, buy twenty bags of rocks and an assortment of shrubs and plants, and spend the morning landscaping my yard, then maybe hike up the hill and back, then bike to the park to catch the sunset. I tend to burn through energy the way some people burn through money; it just doesn't occur to me to save any, and if I have it, I spend it all.

- This is all well and good in the sense that I can be very productive and get a lot done in my energetic phases; but I tend to run my body into the ground or even injure myself, with the result that my energy benders are usually followed by four or five days (or longer) when I can barely move. It is only very recently that I've even begun to entertain the idea that even when I have a lot of energy (energy that can be spent on many exciting projects and adventures, and what are we waiting for!?), I should spend somewhat *less* than my maximum limit—sacrifice that last 20% for the sake of my body, if not for my mind as well.

- When I feel depressed (no quibble with the people in white coats this time!), my body feels very heavy, and my movements slow down quite a bit. Often, I have physical pain—back pain, joint pain, headaches—and it can be hard to tell whether I feel depressed because I'm in pain, or if I'm in pain because I'm feeling down.

- Recent research has shown the existence of fascinating links between physical pain and emotional pain. The more I learned about this, the more I understood the importance of addressing my physical pain in order to curb depression. On days when I have a greater amount of physical pain, I take salt baths, lie on an acupressure mat, and do whatever kind of stretching or self-massage I can to help ease the pain before it curdles into depression.

- My body is kind of a gas guzzler, foodwise. If I go too long without eating, my body basically turns into air, and my mood can drop really suddenly. I find it especially important not to let myself get overly hungry when I'm already depressed or down.

- For me, being too cold is a major trigger for depression, and sometimes when I'm feeling despondent, I'll realize I've been shivering all day. I recently discovered that this is a scientifically proven phenomenon: researchers at the University of Toronto have discovered that people who feel lonely or depressed report feeling colder, and that this feeling can be alleviated by turning up the heat in a room. For this reason, I've started using heat as a therapy for depression: hot baths and showers, warm clothes, or just leaving my chilly house and going to a place I know will be nice and warm.

- I have a very strong tendency to get fevers during or immediately after stressful events, especially events I had complex emotions about (maybe a trip I didn't really want to take, or an obligation I carried out because I didn't see a way out). Sometimes, it feels like my body is literally shutting down to prevent me from doing more things I don't want to do, or to protect me from some feared or unwanted interaction. Gabor Maté writes about this phenomenon in his excellent book *When the Body Says No*.

- I used to see this stressful event $\longrightarrow$ fever pattern as inevitable, but lately I've been experimenting with setting more limits verbally so that my body doesn't have to set them for me, and being more conscious of my emotions generally. For better or for worse, the fevers are a powerful source of information letting me know when I'm not listening, and I expect they will fade away as I get better at saying my own no's.

- Sometimes I wonder if the depression aspect of bipolar is another way the body says no—pulling the rug out from under us so we can't carry out our manic ambitions, letting us know we've blown the limits. I do find that the more conscious I become of my emotions and physical sensations, the less extreme my depression and energy spikes become.

- Whether I feel depressed or agitated, going to a natural environment is almost guaranteed to soothe me. Two hours in the forest or sitting next to the river has a powerful effect on my mind and body, to the point that I use these places as "medicine" at the first sign of depression or stress.

THE MIND: MIRACULOUS FOUNTAIN OF INSIGHT

Your thoughts and beliefs can play a huge role in perpetuating mood cycles. Here are some questions to use as a starting point in exploring this domain:

QUESTIONS TO ASK YOURSELF ABOUT YOUR THOUGHTS:
- What are the recurring thoughts that go through your head when you're depressed? Can you write them down? Do these thoughts hold constant when you're not depressed, or do they seem to disappear?

- Which thoughts go through your head when you feel overwhelmed, anxious, or manic? Can you write them down? Do these thoughts hold constant when you feel happy or normal, or do they disappear?

- Do your depressed/anxious/manic/normal thoughts ever contradict each other? (For example, do you have a recurring thought "I'm a failure" when you feel depressed and "I'm the greatest ever" when you're manic?) Is one more true than the other? Are they both true or not true? Or are they just thoughts with no particular truth-value?

- Can you tell when you're having a "depressed" thought versus a normal thought, a "paranoid" thought versus a normal thought, etc.? Or do all your thoughts seem equally true at all times?

- Do you feel the need to act on all your thoughts? What would happen if you let them pass *without* acting on them? What emotions come up when you refrain from acting on them?

- Do you find it easy to identify your own emotions? Do you ever struggle to name how you're feeling? Do other people ever tell you that you seem depressed, angry, stressed, or manic when you yourself don't feel that way?

- Do you believe you "should" be a certain way? ("I should work harder, I should be happy, I should be more successful . . .") Can you write down a list of your "shoulds"? Do you hold other people to these standards, or do they only apply to you? What do you believe would happen if you didn't achieve these standards? Are the consequences real or imaginary?

- Do you believe yourself to be particularly good or bad, particularly beautiful or ugly, particularly talented or feckless? Does this self-image change depending on your mood?

- How does mood affect your memories? Do you remember different things when you're manic or depressed? Do you *lose* certain memories when you're manic or depressed?

Here are some things I know about my thoughts and beliefs, and how they relate to my moods:

Hilary at time of bipolar diagnosis:

- "My thoughts and beliefs are all true, and any challenge to them is MOST DEFINITELY WRONG."

Current Hilary:

- I have a tendency to set high standards for myself and feel chronically guilty about not attaining them. For me, this has been a big factor in mood cycles: when I have that amazing energy, I get attached to it and start to believe that's how I *should* be all the time: hyperproductive, never-tiring, on the ball. When the crash comes, I feel angry and disappointed that "I" am not that amazing person after all—now I'm just a tired old regular person barely getting through the day. And the next time the energy comes, I'm that much more desperate to grab it and try to maximize it, which results in another crash, and so on and forth.

- If I could learn to be OK with just existing, I'd probably be a lot more happy and stable—but I keep thinking I really *should* be more than a normal person (I should be success-ful! I should be a saint! I should be famous! I should be a successful famous saint! Yeah!) and that contributes to the mood and energy cycles.

- I have a tendency to deny my mood states, at least in their early stages, and feel annoyed with my partner for pointing them out: "I am *not* feeling depressed, why would you say that?" Most of the time, I know perfectly well that I woke up feeling depressed or anxious or agitated—but some puny part of me would rather get mad at him for saying the wrong thing, so that the bad feeling will be *his* fault, rather than admitting I was already feeling terrible before he spoke.

- Denial of emotions and moods can be a major downer in relationships. I think for me, it has something to do with the shame and disappointment I feel for having these unwanted moods—and maybe if I deny having them, or project them onto somebody else, I won't have to feel so bad about myself. One thing that has really helped me with this pattern has been thinking of the various moods and sensations as animals or objects: "Oh, there is this sad-ness-bird perched on my shoulder, hello sadness bird." That way, the moods feel less personal—things that come and go, rather than things I need to get worried or ashamed about.

- My short-term memory is under constant revision. When I'm up, I like to believe I was never down, and when I'm down, I can't seem to remember that I was ever up. If someone tries to give me context or dispute my memory of the previous months and years, I can and do fight them bitterly. I think this pattern is fairly common among people diagnosed with bipolar: when we're manic, we feel like our whole life has been charmed, and when we're depressed, we feel like our entire life has been hell and we might as well die. This trouble with memory is also a contributing factor in the problems some people have with sticking to their medication or other treatment: why go to your counselor when your life is amaaaazing (never mind the fact that you were suicidal the month before); why do your meditation practice when life's not worth living anyway (never mind the fact that just last week you were marveling at the exquisite sweetness of the ducklings at the Chinese garden).

SOCIAL INTERACTIONS: ALSO A MIRACULOUS FOUNTAIN OF INSIGHT

Mental health and illness don't exist in a vacuum. Unless you are a legitimate hermit, you are going to be around people in some capacity, and those interactions can have a huge impact on your mental state.

QUESTIONS TO ASK YOURSELF ABOUT SOCIAL INTERACTIONS:

- Do you enjoy being around people? Are you an introvert, an extrovert, or somewhere in between? Do you prefer to socialize one on one or in groups? Are there social situations that make you feel stressed or anxious?

- How do social interactions affect your sleep and energy levels? Do you have insomnia after social gatherings? Do parties stimulate mania or depression? Do you become more or less aware of your stress levels when you're around other people? Do you feel comfortable asserting your own needs and feelings, or do you find yourself doing whatever it takes to fit in?
- Do you feel like yourself around other people, or do you change into a different person? How can you tell when you're not being yourself?
- How does mania/hypomania change your interactions with people? Do you make more commitments, make promises you can't deliver on, get into more arguments, say things you wouldn't normally say, become more charming and talkative than you normally are?
- How does depression affect your social interactions? Do you isolate yourself; start fights with your family, friends, or partner; skip out on commitments; or drop activities?
- Do any particular patterns of interaction work better for you? Do you need recovery time after an intensely social day? Or do you thrive on social interaction and become depressed when you don't get enough of it?

Here are some things I've observed about my interactions with other people, and how this plays into my moods:

Hilary at time of bipolar diagnosis:

- "Other people? So not a problem. Deeeefinitely not a problem. In fact, I love it when my roommates throw huge parties with lots of strangers. I'm just going to hide in my room and smoke this weed now."

Current Hilary:

- I am pretty introverted. For me, social interactions range from mildly taxing to utterly exhausting, a few very special people excepted. It's not that I don't enjoy talking to people—I do—but I enjoy it the way I enjoy playing basketball: it's stimulating, but tiring, and I wouldn't want to do it all day, and on days when I'm exhausted for other reasons, I barely want to do it at all. Sometimes it's tempting to cut my social interactions down to the bare minimum or even become a hermit. Yet research suggests that both mental and physical health are profoundly linked to meaningful social connections, and outcomes for people with depression, bipolar, and other conditions are usually better when they stay connected to other people.

- After lots of trial and error, I have become pretty good at identifying which kinds of social activities stress me out and trigger exhaustion, and which ones energize me and keep me afloat. I've discovered I prefer to interact with people around a shared interest (in my case, practicing music) or volunteer work (copyediting and habitat restoration) rather than noisy parties or "fun" group activities that usually aren't so fun. When I was in college, I tried to force myself to get into these "fun" activities, usually by drinking, because I didn't understand why they were so unpleasant to me. Now I've come to accept my lack of interest in normal-person socializing, rather than feeling like it is something that needs to be fixed or overcome.

- When I am in an up phase, I tend to overestimate my desire and ability to be around people. I'll accept too many invitations or make plans or offers that later seem unrealistic or even catastrophic ("Wait, did I really just agree to host that acquaintance at my house for three weeks? I take it back, I take it back!"). When the up phase is over, I find myself with all sorts of commitments I either have to honor or undo. My inability to follow through on the (in hindsight, extravagant) social offers I made when I was feeling great make me feel guilty and ashamed.

- On the flip side, when I feel depressed, I tend to overestimate the degree to which social interactions will be intolerable: "I should get out of the house, but I just couldn't handle running into anybody." This can lead me to isolate myself, when in fact a social interaction at just the right time can jolt me *out* of depression. I have found it helpful to have a few commitments that put me in contact with people throughout the week (volunteering on Wednesday afternoons, music practice Monday nights) which ensure that I get a certain base level of social vitamins, even if I don't seek out other interactions.

- Although I resist his insights a lot of the time, living with my partner has been a great source of learning and support. He can often tell when I'm in a mood before I can; and his presence day by day and year by year provides a sort of big-picture stability, even when things feel less stable in a given week or month. The things we argue about are most often the things we need most to learn from each other (he likes to sit in the sun and relax; I hate sitting still and relaxing! Guess what I need to do more of?)

MORE ABOUT INSIGHT

As you become more and more aware of the things your mind and body are doing, you will begin to see patterns that will help you take care of yourself. ("I always get cold when I'm depressed, and taking a bath always helps" "I always invite twenty house guests when I'm feeling hyphy, and I always regret it later.")

You will also start to notice contradictions—places where your mind and body seem to disagree:

Mind says: "Parties are fun, right? College students love parties, and I'm a college student, therefore I must love parties."

Body says: "I don't like the noise and crowdedness! Headache, headache!"

Mind says: "Winston is such a nice person. I should really hang out with him."

Body says: "I don't really enjoy being around Winston. I feel achy and exhausted."

Mind says: "I have so much energy today. I should definitely take advantage of this to knock twenty tasks off my to-do list (preferably twenty tasks involving chain saws)."

Body says: "I'd be happier going for a walk by the river. The trees there are so nice!"

In modern societies, people tend to get stuck in their heads—listening to what they think they *should* do or be, rather than to how they actually feel. By paying more attention to your physical sensations (hot, cold, achy, wired, tired, easy breathing or shallow breathing, etc.), you can develop an early-detection system for stress. And by developing an early-detection system for stress, you can head off mood cycles before they get too big to handle.

I am a sour and curmudgeonly person, and bristle at any sort of "exercise" suggested in books like this one. However, if you are a more willing and good-natured person than me, you may find it useful to start a written list of discoveries, large and small, that you make about yourself and your moods. The next time you feel depression creeping in, seize it as a valuable opportunity—"Ah, the leopard is here! What is it doing this time?" Then make notes: "Mood dropped an hour after eating donuts, body chilly." "Bad feelings, most intense in the afternoon, lifted at sunset." "Dang leopard peed on the couch again, must evict." It might not seem that helpful at first, but over the course of a year, you will start to notice patterns. If you realize that you always feel terrible in the afternoon, but better in the evening, the next shitty afternoon won't terrify you so much—you know you just have to wait for the sun to go down, and the feeling will go down with it.

This kind of knowledge is what distinguishes seasoned jungle guides from inexperienced trekkers. They're in the same jungle, with the same leopards—but whereas the greenhorns run around in a panic whenever they hear a rustling in the bush, the experienced guides are experts on leopard behavior, and this knowledge helps them think clearly, make good decisions, and distinguish a rustling bush from a real, live leopard encounter. The good news is, we can all become experienced guides through our own jungles—it just takes a little bit of time, patience, and practice.

6

NINJA SKILLS FOR THE MENTALLY CHILL
TOOLS FOR STAYING SANE

The more closely you learn to observe yourself, the sooner you can recognize the signs of depression, anxiety, and incipient agitation or mania and work with them before they gain momentum. Tending your mind is a little like tending a garden: if you're not very attuned to what's going on, waist-high weeds can seem to appear "out of nowhere," healthy plants appear to die "for no reason," and trees that were "just fine" the day before are "suddenly" infested with tiny white beetles. To an inexperienced gardener, all these disasters seem to come on suddenly and for no apparent reason, requiring all sorts of emergency measures to remediate.

On the other hand, an experienced gardener pulls out the weeds while they're still tiny, gives the plants water and mulch *before* they wilt, and both notices and addresses the beetle eggs before they have a chance to hatch. Because this gardener deals with problems while they are still small, she rarely needs to resort to emergency measures or to break her back pulling up six-foot monster weeds.

At the time I was diagnosed with bipolar, I had so little awareness of my body or stress levels that I literally had to be sobbing before I realized I was sad, or be awake for three nights running before I realized I was stressed and anxious. Learning to "hear" my body and mind has been a revelation for me, and a crucial part of my stability. The following ninja skills are all most effective when they're applied *early*—not when you're already in the thick of an episode. But hey, that's what you develop insight for!

Here are some things to do when you realize you're sliding into depression, anxiety, or mania:

NINJA SKILL #1: TARGET YOUR BODY.

People with bipolar and depression hear so much about brain chemistry that it's easy to believe that all mood problems are best addressed through the brain—by taking more medications or thinking different thoughts. But mental ninjas know that a very sneaky way to reach the mind is through the body, and you can encourage your mood to change by changing what you're doing with your body.

The link between posture and depression is well established, yet most people don't think of postural adjustment as a first-line strategy against the early signs of depression. This is too bad, because adjusting your posture is a gentle, free, and highly effective way to head off depressive feelings before they "settle in" and become full depression. Simply standing or sitting with your shoulders back and head aligned can bring on a feeling of confidence and strength, replacing the defeated slump of depression. For those of you who are rolling your eyes, this is not mere hippie shit: a 2015 study on posture and mood published in *Health Psychology* concluded:

> Adopting an upright seated posture in the face of stress can maintain self-esteem, reduce negative mood, and increase positive mood compared to a slumped posture . . . Sitting upright may be a simple behavioral strategy to help build resilience to stress. The research is consistent with embodied cognition theories that *muscular and autonomic states influence emotional responding.* [emphasis added]

In other words, your body has a direct effect on your mood. And if you'd like to adjust your mood, adjusting your posture is a completely reasonable way to undertake it.

Posture is not the only way you can affect your mood via your body. Vigorous exercise such as walking, running, or swimming has such a tremendous impact on mood and sleep that many doctors now prescibe a daily hike or lap swim long before they'll agree to prescribe meds for depression and insomnia. The rhythm of sustained exercise is soothing, and gentle, persistant motion in the physical world appears to get things unstuck in the emotional world. One of the best things a depression-prone person can do is to find a running/swimming/cycling buddy for daily (yes, daily!) sessions. An hour a day in the water or on the trail is a highly effective therapy, and it will help you feel better in both the short and long term.

NINJA SKILL #2: WIDEN YOUR FOCUS.

Mania is often accompanied by an increase in so-called goal-directed activities (see also the aforementioned twenty tasks involving chainsaws). There's a feeling of pressure—a burning need to use up every last drop of energy and not let it go to waste—and a feeling of extreme urgency ("if I don't do all my chainsaw projects today, I might never get them done, and that would be *INTOL-ERABLE*"). All this can lead to a sort of tunnel vision ("chainsaw projects! must do chainsaw projects")—a narrowing of focus to the exclusion of other things.

Therefore, when you notice yourself entering this sort of tunnel, pause and **widen your focus**. What is your body doing? What is the weather doing? What is your boyfriend talking about, whom you tuned out because you were thinking about the twenty projects you need to get started on? What does your food taste like? What does your dog smell like? What do your shoes feel like?

This doesn't mean you have to stuff down your desire to engage in, ahem, goal-directed activity, or pretend that the desire isn't there. But actively and consciously maintaining awareness of your body and of the outside world can act as a sort of anchor, reminding you that your obsessive desire isn't the whole of reality, and the world will continue to exist if you don't follow the urge to act.

Widening your focus is also very useful for depression, anxiety, or any other feeling or impulse than can seem to hog all your mental attention. If you are able to "share" your mental attention with your body, your dog, the clouds in the sky, and the pavement under your feet, instead of giving it all to your depressive thought, your depression will have that much less to feed on. Again, it's not a matter of trying to delete the depressive feeling or pretend it isn't there, but to put it in the context of a wider field, instead of giving it a singular claim on your attention.

Try this. The next time you realize your attention is being monopolized by a depressive loop or a manic urge, stop whatever you're doing and take a little inventory of the universe: "Yes, an urge to do chainsaw projects is there. And also, there is a chirping bird and the smell of baking bread and a funny red sock and a train going past and a tree with its branches waving in the wind." Every time your mind snaps back to the obsessive thought or feeling, gently repeat the process—not to distract yourself from the urge or cover it up, but to keep it in the context of wider reality.

NINJA SKILL #3: BREAK IT DOWN.

I once read about a technique for surviving torture that is practiced by Zen monks. The technique involves breaking down each moment into smaller and smaller moments, so that one only has to survive one micro-moment at a time. Staying in the hyper-present, the mind has less of a chance to get overwhelmed by fear and horror.

Some months after reading this, I went through a very difficult time. My body and mind were in such agony it really felt like torture. I remembered the Zen technique and began to practice it: breaking down each seemingly fixed unit of time into the smallest units I could perceive. While I am no means a master of this approach, I found that even my clumsy attempts at focusing on the hyper-present were very helpful in making cracks in the apparently solid wall of pain and suffering I was experiencing.

When a person is in a lot of mental or physical pain, the pain can appear to be fixed and constant, dominating everything. You feel terrible existing; there doesn't seem to be any part of your life that isn't infected by the pain. The practice of breaking down time into tiny units keeps your mind from panicking at the enormity of the problem, while poking unexpected breathing holes into what otherwise seems impenetrable. It is a variation on the idea of widening your focus described above: by radically expanding the number of individual moments you perceive, you cannot get too attached to any single sensation.

Here's a simple experiment to get you started. Pick an activity you would normally treat as a single action, such as climbing the stairs or filling a cup of water. Now, see how many individual moments you can perceive within that "single" action: *water falling into bottom of cup, wind from open window is touching my face, water making splashing sound, water rising, I am inhaling, stomach gurgling while water rises, bird flies past window while water rises, sun sparkling on surface of water, I swallow, reaching to turn off tap, lift my foot slightly, muscles tensing in forearm, fingers touching cool of metal spigot, fingers gripping around spigot, holding cold glass in other hand, sensation of wetness, bringing cup away from sink . . .* This is a very short example—in its complete form, the simple act of filling a cup with water could fill many pages of "moments."

As you practice this technique, you slowly discover that what seemed like a constant wall of suffering actually has shape and texture. Maybe you felt depression when the cup was starting to fill, but you realize the depression blinked out for a micro-second when you noticed the sunlight on the surface of the water. Even if your overall sensation is still "depressed," you realize there are plenty of previously unnoticed moments when other sensations are present. And for someone who is deep in the hole of depression, even a half-second of something other than depression can be a lifesaver—the trick is to *notice* that half-second.

NINJA SKILL #4: QUESTION YOUR UNQUESTIONABLES.

When you're anxious or in distress, every thought that goes through your mind can seem totally real and true. You can get so wrapped up in your own thoughts you don't even realize there are a million other possible ways of responding to the same situation.

I suffered from extreme insomnia for years. In a desperate attempt to deal with it, I developed all sorts of rigid rules about sleep: I *had* to get to bed by midnight or I wouldn't fall asleep, there couldn't be *any* light or noise, and if I got less than seven hours of sleep, I was going to be screwed the next day. I responded to any threat to these rules with self-righteous anger: I was *right* about sleep! My sleeping rules were validated by medical science! They were completely unquestionable!

This obsession with so-called sleep hygiene drove my partner insane. "If you want to learn how to sleep," he'd say, "take your cue from people who are good sleepers. Stop reading books by *bad* sleepers."

Then one night, my friend Max crashed at our house with his band when they were on tour. When Max was ready to sleep, he just sprawled out on the living room floor and went to sleep—he didn't wait for everybody else to go to bed, or the lights to be off, or anything to change. My partner's advice finally made sense to me: Max was a good sleeper, and Max didn't give a flying fuck about sleep hygiene. I shouldn't be more careful and obsessive about sleep—I should be more like Max!

In the weeks and months that followed, I started copying Max. I stopped "going to bed" (with its elaborate rituals of stressing out and watching the clock). When I was tired, I merely sprawled out on the floor or the couch without even changing out of my clothes. I didn't go to bed "on time"—I lay down if and when I felt tired, whether that was at eight o'clock in the evening or three o'clock in the morning. I used to treat my sleep like something incredibly fragile, but it turned out I needed to do exactly the opposite: I had to send myself a strong message that sleep was something easy and automatic and not a big deal. Sleep had become an "unquestionable" topic for me, and it didn't improve until I took it off its pedestal and questioned it.

If you want to learn to sleep, study people who are good at sleeping. If you want to be less anxious, study people who are low anxiety. If you want to manage your emotions better, study people who ride things out calmly. How do their beliefs and attitudes differ from yours? How does their posture differ from yours? Can you steal any of those ninja skills from them? How are your beliefs (i.e. "I am fragile") keeping you stuck in a less-useful pattern?

NINJA SKILL #5: PRACTICE ACCEPTANCE.

Acceptance is a contradictory idea. For example, take a thing you really, really don't like—such as depression. You want this very bad, no good thing to go away. Shouldn't you do everything you can to fight it, reject it, even deny its existence?

Yet paradoxically, accepting an unpleasant sensation like depression can be the first step in reducing its power. Here's why: if you immediately try to make something go away, you are sending yourself a message that this thing is unbearable, a disaster, a really big threat that must be acted upon right away. If, however, you can sit with the bad feeling and just *watch* it for a while, you might realize that it's not as powerful as you thought. It's fangs aren't as sharp as you imagined, and its eyes aren't as scary.

Until you can do this, depression is never just depression. It's always depression *plus* fear of being depressed forever *plus* disappointment at being depressed *plus* anxiety that everyone hates you for being so depressed *plus* a million other thoughts and feelings that come up around the original feeling of depression. If you can cut down on all these peripheral forms of suffering, the experience of depression will automatically be that much less awful. And the way to cut down on the peripheral stuff is to accept the depression exactly as it is—to feel it and watch it, without denying any aspect of its existence or getting unduly worried about what it means.

The other day, I found a drowned rat in a water tub in my backyard. Dealing with this problem was actually very simple (scoop rat out with a shovel, tie it in a plastic bag, put it in the garbage—a one-minute operation). But I compounded the simple problem of the drowned rat by piling other problems and worries onto it: What if there are other rats? What if my neighbors saw the rat? What if there is a plague of rats and we have to fight them off with pointy sticks? This wouldn't have happened if I hadn't forgotten to close the compost bin! I'm a bad person! I'm a failure! Everyone hates me! My life is a disaster!

I ended up avoiding the dead rat all day, or telling myself I was avoiding it, but really I felt anxious and upset—even if I could convince my mind there was no rat, my body knew otherwise. When I finally confronted the dead rat, I realized how much I'd compounded my problem by trying to avoid it: if I had just scooped out the rat when I first saw it, I wouldn't have had to feel stressed and worried for more than a minute, let alone for an entire day.

The same is true of depression. We often want to deny the existence of "negative" emotions—*oops, let's pretend I didn't see that.* But if it's there, it's there, and denying it is only going to drain mental energy. Even if it's unpleasant (and what could be more unpleasant than a drowned rat?), it's always better to confront it and deal with it.

Therefore, when you feel something you'd rather not feel, like depression or manic agitation, stop what you're doing and *just feel it*. Say to yourself, "I see you, depression!" It's already there, so you're not going to make it any worse by acknowledging it any more than I made the dead rat appear by noticing it in the water tub. Next, accept that there are aspects of it you find unpleasant: "I'd really rather not feel depressed. But since I do, I'm going to take good care of the situation." Maintaining awareness of the reality of the situation, you can take appropriate steps to feel better.

NINJA SKILL #6: RUN YOUR OWN EXPERIMENTS.

Like many people diagnosed with bipolar, I have been through periods when the suffering of life seemed unbearable, to the point that I have questioned whether it was worth living at all. During one such period, I had been in such pain for so long that I couldn't even pretend to be coping anymore. "I don't want you to kill yourself," I said to myself, "But how about you practice being dead? Maybe that will work almost as well as actually *being* dead."

It was the middle of the day. There was sun coming in through the window. I lay down on the living room floor and committed myself to being dead. Cars passed outside, and I felt my aversion to the engines rising up. But then I remembered that the traffic on the street wasn't my problem anymore—I was dead! A few moments later, some of my regular worry loops started playing—

"I never wrote back to so-and-so, I never finished writing that essay . . ."—but then I remembered something incredible: I was dead! I didn't have to finish my to-do list or solve my problems.

As I lay there practicing being dead, something amazing happened: I started to feel better. A *lot* better. For the first time in months, I was able to let thoughts and sensations arise and pass without committing to them. It was like shrugging off a winter coat of worries and thought-loops and realizing the coat wasn't actually me.

Far from being a morbid gesture, practicing being dead gave me a fresh perspective on life. I recovered from my depression soon after. It later occurred to me that this practice had a lot in common with the "corpse pose" practiced in every yoga class—maybe they were even the same thing. But while I would have rolled my eyes at the idea of practicing corpse pose, I was willing to practice being dead because it was "my" idea.

If you, like me, are resistant to trying out ideas you read in books or hear from other people, run your own experiments and devise your own practices. You just might stumble upon something that really helps you, exactly when you need it.

LAST THOUGHTS ON NINJA SKILLS

These are just a small handful of ways you can work with your moods and bipolar symptoms. As you develop more insight into who you are and how you tick, you will figure out your own personal set of ninja skills—and the ninja skills you figure out for yourself are going to be way, way better than anything a book can tell you.

Practicing ninja skills does not necessarily mean that you can eliminate *all* suffering and *all* mood changes from your life, or that you will never need medication or counseling or acupuncture or a chocolate donut or a hug from your Grandma ever again (at least, not until you are some kind of highly enlightened *super* ninja). In fact, a big part of mental chillness is accepting that you are not a perfect person, and you're gonna do some things you probably shouldn't do, make some decisions you probably would have made differently if you'd really stopped to think about them, and have some feelings you'd rather not have.

What insight *does* do is give you a broader perspective and a greater understanding of yourself and your life so that you can gradually stop making the same mistakes (and make new ones instead!) and clinging to the thoughts and behaviors that really aren't helping you. Sure, your life will still involve a lot of suffering—most lives do—but maybe, just maybe, it will involve more peacefulness too.

7

BUGS IN THE JUNGLE
SUICIDE, PSYCH WARDS, AND OTHER DOWNERS

Let's face it: this is a self-help book (or it's at least pretending to be one), and the job of self-help books is to tell you that your whole life can be fabulous, amazing, *awesome,* if you just do what they say (in this case, learning self-observation, making lifestyle adjustments, and taking a thoughtful approach to medication). But the truth is, bipolar disorder can be a very powerful opponent, and life isn't always set up to support your well-being. (Remember that cabin in the woods, with the masseuse and the groovy therapist and the bicycle? Still waiting for that to come about!) Even if you do your best to manage your bipolar symptoms *perfectly*—be the perfect med-taker or the perfect lifestyle-adjuster or the perfect positive-thinker or the perfect all-of-the-above—there are still gonna be bumps in the road. Although they certainly don't happen to everyone diagnosed with bipolar disorder, things like suicide attempts, hospitalizations, and recurring episodes of mania or depression are real-life tarantulas lurking in the jungle of bipolar disorder (and in plenty of other jungles too). Looking them in the face is the first step to diminishing their power. (Side note: why can't more jungles be stocked with bunnies?)

SUICIDE

When you go hiking in the Rockies, there are posters at the trailheads telling you what to do if you encounter a grizzly bear. I always read these posters avidly, because as a frequent hiker, I would really, really like some solid instructions on what to do if this happened to me. Yet time after time I'm frustrated: the instructions are always vague, saying things like "stay calm" and "leave the area." Leave the area? What if there's another bear behind me? I've questioned rangers about this, and after reciting the usual Grizzly Bear Protocol, they shrug and say, "You just have to think on your feet."

Feeling suicidal is like having a grizzly bear encounter. Everybody has some general idea of what you should do if you feel suicidal ("leave the area!"), but when you get down to specific variables ("But what if there are *two* bears?"), it becomes obvious that nobody has a fucking clue. It's a scary, high-stakes, high-risk situation, and you're just gonna have to work with whatever you can grab (which is hopefully a telephone or your best friend's hand).

The stats on bipolar and suicide are terrible (and wildly variant). The quotes are all over the map. You can find stats claiming that anywhere from 10 to 50 percent of people with bipolar disorder attempt suicide. Seriously, guys? Fifty percent? Then you find out that their test pool consisted of a thousand recently bankrupt, grief-stricken, rapid-cycling sixty-year-olds on their fortieth hospitalization. Maybe *that* test pool has a 50 percent likelihood of attempting suicide. Attempting—not even completing. Another test pool might have a 20 percent likelihood of attempting suicide. For another test pool, it might be 15 percent.

Don't trust statistics. Statistics know nothing about you. That being said, having bipolar disorder does place you at a higher risk of suicide than the general population, and there are certain factors within bipolar that can place you at an even higher risk. I've decided to edit out the numbers ("eating pudding makes you two point twelve times as likely") because the whole point of this book is to make you feel less like a human scorecard and more like a human. But here are the risk factors themselves:

- *Frequency of hospitalization*
  The biggest factor associated with suicide attempts among people with bipolar disorder is being hospitalized several times. If you've been in and out of the hospital several times, you're more likely to attempt suicide at some point. This is why it's important to take all the measures you can to stay stable—so that you can go through the psychiatric wringer as few times as humanly possible.
- *Depressive or mixed first episode*
  If your first episode was depressive or mixed, your risk of attempting suicide is higher than if your first episode was manic or hypomanic.
- *Stressful life events before the onset of bipolar disorder*
  If the onset of your bipolar disorder was precipitated by a gnarly life event, like physical abuse, you have a higher risk of attempting suicide.

- *Episodes occurring without downtime in between*

  If you have episode after episode after episode with no symptom-free intervals in between, then—you guessed it!—you have a higher risk of attempting suicide. That psychiatric wringer can wear a person out pretty fast.

- *Drug and alcohol abuse*

  Don't abuse drugs and alcohol, kids. It raises your risk of acting on impulses, which raises your risk of attempting suicide.

- *Family history*

  If you have bipolar disorder *and* a family member who committed suicide, your risk of attempting suicide is higher than the general population. It's like alcoholism: if your parents were alcoholics, you're genetically at risk for developing alcoholism yourself.

More general, non-bipolar-specific risk factors for suicide include loneliness and social isolation, physical illness or chronic pain, cultural or religious beliefs that validate or glorify suicide, and recent loss (losing your house, your job, your significant other, your social status, etc.).

Now, other than doing whatever you can to get stable and avoid mood episodes, all this might make it seem like suicide risk is something largely outside your control. After all, you don't get to decide whether or not to suffer a major loss, whether to have a suicide-prone family, or whether your first mood episode was depressive. But even if you have every single one of those out-of-your-control risk factors, don't despair: there is also such a thing as *protective* factors, and pumping these up can help insulate you from suicide.

SUICIDE PROTECTIVE FACTORS

For some reason, the factors that lower your risk of suicide never get as much attention as the risk factors. This is too bad, because when you read over the protective factors (perhaps with the help of a friend or counselor), you realize there are all sorts of ways of lowering your suicide risk, and most of them are good for your general health and happiness too. The University of Western Michigan has a great list of these on their website; here are a few that jumped out at me (notes and comments are my own).[1]

- Attitudes, values, and norms prohibiting suicide, e.g., strong beliefs about the meaning and value of life; Cultural, religious or spiritual beliefs that discourage suicide

I once met a Buddhist who suffered from serious bouts of depression. He talked about what a relief it would be to die—but said that, unfortunately, suicide was not an option for him because he believed he would merely be reincarnated and start suffering all over again. While I found this conversation heartbreaking, it was also fascinating: here was a person whose cultural norms and religious beliefs were acting as a powerful prevention to suicide. For him, the meaning of life was to escape the wheel of rebirth—and suicide was not an effective strategy for doing this.

I'm not saying everyone with bipolar should become a Buddhist just to lower their suicide risk—but finding something to believe in is a powerful antidote to the suicide urge. Maybe you don't believe in reincarnation . . .

---

1   *https://wmich.edu/suicideprevention/basics/protective*

but you strongly believe your life has a meaning and purpose you haven't discovered yet, and you need to stick around to figure it out.

- Responsibilities and duties to others

Having other people count on you can be stressful—but *not* having responsibilities towards other people can be a sign that you're socially isolated, a risk factor for depression and suicide. I've experienced this firsthand: my boyfriend and I were nomadic for years, traveling from place to place without a fixed home, and while I enjoyed the adventure, the lack of being *useful* really got to me. When we settled in Portland for a few years, I was relieved to be in a place where I could take on responsibilities—volunteer work, music rehearsals—that would integrate me with other people and help me feel like I really existed. These days, I think twice about going on vacation (much less eliminating myself from the planet) because I don't want to miss out on my responsibilities.

- Pets

The Buddhist I mentioned earlier explained that he would not commit suicide because of his beliefs about the nature of reincarnation; I have also met people who would not commit suicide because of their dog or cat. A friend of mine got a puppy while still in college, even though circumstances made it highly impractical for her to own one; she was recovering from a severe bout of depression and explained that the puppy all but forced her to exercise, play, express love, and do other things to keep the depression from taking over again. A suicideprevention puppy or cat is a wonderful thing indeed, and something that many people with and without mental illnesses have discovered independently.

- Strong connections to friends and family as well as supportive significant others

"But wait," you say, "One of the main reasons I feel suicidal is because I have no friends and my family is a nightmare. How am I supposed to benefit from this protective factor?"

Find a new family, even if it's temporary. The point is to have some kind of strong, regular social connection—the whole "blood relative" thing is a far second. Maybe your family is Alcoholics Anonymous, the Juggalos, the Hare Krishna, the Buddhists, the Christians, the Unitarians, the cat adoption people, the ukulele people, or the Dungeons and Dragons weirdos. At some point, it doesn't even matter. (I mean—it sort of matters. Plenty of cults want to be your "family" and it's probably a bad idea—but if it's your only alternative to suicide, well . . .)

If possible, you can also work on strengthening relationships to "actual" family members, but that's a topic for a different book.

- Opportunities to participate in and contribute to school or community projects and activities

This one is pretty self-explanatory: Volunteer! Join! Show up! Take on a role! It sounds dorky (and it can even *feel* dorky), but it does work. And if you live in a place where there's not much to participate in or show up for, find an online community to hang out in. Again, we're talking suicide prevention, not best-case scenarios—so if acting as a moderator on the Mini Donkey Fans of America forum is the only "community project" you've got going, hey, it's better than nothing.

DEALING WITH SUICIDAL THOUGHTS

The first thing you should do if you have suicidal thoughts (doctors call this "ideation") is to talk to your psychiatrist, if you have one (or to whoever your go-to counselor or mentor happens to be, if you don't). Suicidal thoughts are sometimes a side effect of psychiatric drugs, and you might need a change in your medications. And if your suicidal thoughts *aren't* a side effect, that's all the more reason to get help immediately. Don't be embarrassed or squeamish. If the brakes on your car stopped working, you wouldn't sit around dithering whether they're broken *enough* to warrant a check-in with the mechanic. Ditto thoughts of suicide.

If you feel actively suicidal (i.e., imminently about to kill yourself), holler at everyone you possibly can and ask them for help. Get on the crisis telephone line and talk to a counselor (1-800-273-TALK), call your psychiatrist if you have one, and get your mom or uncle or best friend or neighbor to drive over and pick you up. You can even go to the emergency room or call 911. There is an unbelievably huge and passionate and loving suicide-prevention community out there; they care about you, and it would make their friggin' day to save your life. So please let them.

The most important things when you're feeling suicidal are to (a) call people who can help you and (b) not be alone. Whatever you do, don't start drinking or taking drugs to help you deal with your suicidal thoughts, because these things will only make you more likely to act on them. It's a good idea to keep a list of emergency phone numbers in your wallet or in your cell phone contacts list so you don't need to scramble to find them when it's down to the wire. Remember that suicidal thoughts are a symptom of your disorder; they are not real, normal thoughts. Feeling suicidal is like having a heart attack or running into a grizzly bear when you're hiking: it's not your fault; it's just something that's *out there*.

ONE WAY OF UNDERSTANDING SUICIDAL THOUGHTS

Think of it this way.

Suicidal thoughts are a symptom of bipolar. Bipolar is a medical condition, like having a cold, and the symptoms of bipolar are like coughs and a runny nose. Even though it feels more intimate and personal, suicidal ideation is just as impersonal as chills and a fever. When the episode clears up, it clears up (and if it doesn't, you should tell your psychiatrist). Suicidal thoughts can be very scary, and if you think of them this way—as a symptom, as a trick your mind is playing on you as part of a disease—you can place them in a less scary context.

When I was really depressed in Vancouver, I had recurring thoughts of filling my backpack with rocks, taking a lot of Seroquel, and jumping off the Burrard Street Bridge. I think the logic was that I would be too sleepy to notice I was drowning. What helped me get through that time was understanding those thoughts metaphorically—as a painful, hacking cough that was a completely impersonal symptom of depression, nothing more. People who meditate love this stuff; they call it detachment. The thinking goes that you can peacefully observe negative thoughts and sensations without making them personal, and by not getting involved with them, you don't get hurt by them.

Example:
Old thought: "I'm so depressed. This grief is unbearable. Every moment is a living death. I want to die."

Detached thought: "Ah, it appears I am experiencing grief! Hello, grief. It appears I am having thoughts of suicide! Hello, thoughts of suicide."

By practicing this kind of thinking, you can help yourself disarm the power of suicidal thoughts and other negative emotions—at least enough to survive until you're able to get further help. You establish that *you* are not the same thing as your thoughts, and you are not subject to suffering from them. It takes practice and isn't a replacement for medication or the support of a doctor (until you become a fully enlightened being, that is), but it can do you lots of good. Practicing detachment helps you realize that your pain isn't permanent, and you, therefore, don't need the permanent solution of suicide to get rid of it.

"SO WHAT HAPPENS IF I ATTEMPT SUICIDE?"

Well, for starters you could die. And as much fun as that sounds, I'm not coming after you. (Actually, I will, eventually, but this is neither here nor there.)

If you don't die, you'll be found or stopped by somebody and taken to the emergency room. This is what goes down when you go to the emergency room following a suicide attempt:

The emergency-room staff stabilize you physically (by pumping your stomach, extracting the bullet from your chest, sewing up your arms, etc.) and emotionally (by sedating you). They do tests to see if you're drunk, on street drugs, or on medication that might be causing a suicidal side effect. Next, you'll go through a mental-health assessment, where they'll try to figure out how crazy you are, whether your craziness is acute or chronic, whether you have previous suicide attempts, and why you tried to commit suicide this time. You, your family, and the doctors will talk about treatment options and support systems that are available to you. Next, the emergency-department personnel will decide if you need to be hospitalized, either of your own free will or by having you committed. If they decide to have you committed, a legal process will ensue that will take from three to ten days. If they decide you don't need to be hospitalized, you'll be sent home with a plan to check in with your doctor regularly and stay away from guns and knives.

"WHAT'S IT LIKE CALLING A CRISIS TELEPHONE LINE?"

Crisis telephone lines are staffed by counselors or trained volunteers whose job it is to get you through your immediate crisis and point you towards further help. If you're calling because you feel suicidal, the person who answers will listen to you, reflect your problems back to you, and encourage you to keep talking and stay on the line. At the end of the call, she'll refer you to a service in your area, such as a drop-in crisis center or clinic you can go to.

Oh yeah, you don't have to be on the verge of suicide to call. These peeps are there for you *whenever*. You can call them to cry about breaking up with Steve. They won't hang up on you. If you don't have a psychiatrist to call, a crisis phone line is a good bet, because the act of calling is in itself a diversion from whatever destruction you're about to wreak. Check out the Resources section for crisis lines in the United States and Canada.

DRUGZ 'N' BOOZE

Tons of people with bipolar disorder self-medicate with drugs and alcohol, and this often turns into addiction that makes bipolar even harder to treat.

Why do we turn to drugs and alcohol in the first place, and why are we more prone to developing addictions? What are our reasons for using drugs and alcohol to self-medicate?

ALCOHOL REASONS
Here are some ideas:

> "It's my friend's wedding and I need to have a good time or at least seem happy."
>
> "I want to lift my depression."
>
> "I need to sleep."
>
> "I need to relax."
>
> "I'm anxious around people, and alcohol helps me have fun."
>
> "I need to shut off my brain/slow down my racing thoughts/ escape from the world."
>
> "I want to cut loose and be myself."

These are all totally valid human desires. Who *doesn't* want some relief from their suffering, some escape from their fears and anxieties, some permission to be a version of themselves they don't normally allow themselves to be? The problem isn't that these are bad or unreasonable things to want. The problem isn't even that alcohol and other mind-altering substances are inherently bad, in the right amount and in the right context. Used thoughtfully, almost anything can be a tool for positive growth. But the whole point of a tool is that you put it down when it's done its job, and the problem with drugs and alcohol is that too many people hold onto the tool, finding more and more uses for it, long after it's achieved its original purpose.

Bipolar disorder often has alcohol or drug abuse as a prominent feature. Whether this is because people with bipolar have a genetic predisposition to addiction and alcoholism, or because the symptoms of bipolar tend to make you *want* to drink (see also, "I need to shut my brain off!") or because people diagnosed with mental illnesses are more likely to live in chaotic environments or be traumatized in a way that makes temporary numbness appealing, it's hard to say for sure (probably all of the above). It seems reasonable that the same things that help prevent suicide (meaning, purpose, positive social relationships, community involvement, self-worth, physical health) will also have a protective effect on addictions—in other words, the more you can cultivate those positive forces, the less you will want or need to turn to drugs and alcohol for relief. It goes without saying that mere willpower is not enough to overcome a dependency—if those protective factors are not in place, and continually reaffirmed, it can be almost impossible to stay away from drugs or alcohol. Building up and maintaining those protective factors should be an ongoing process in every person-with-bipolar's life.

This is not an addictions-and-recovery book, and I am not an addictions expert (or an *anything* expert, come to think of it). If alcoholism or drug addiction are a part of your bipolar landscape, Alcoholics Anonymous and other programs are there for you, and you deserve to access them.

PSYCH WARDS

You don't have to go further than the local library or bookstore to find accounts of life in the psych ward. Accounts of hospitalization for mental illness are often poeticized, dramatized, and scandalized—and with good reason. Crazy shit goes down in psych wards—that's what psych wards are *for*—but not crazy in the fun way. People who have been there will tell you very firmly that you do *not* want to be hospitalized. It's not glamorous, sexy, or fun in any way. It won't give you mystique or higher cred with your bipolar homeboys or homegirls. Doctors hate hospitalizing people, especially young people, because a one-week hospitalization can set you back an entire year.

Being hospitalized for mania or depression can be a terrifying experience. You've lost control; you're not allowed to leave, not allowed to make decisions in the usual way. Unless you're someplace really fancy, chances are the hospital is a pretty unpleasant place, full of harsh lights, beeping machines, ugly furniture, and total strangers you can't really get away from—remind me

Joshua Walters, now a popular mental-health speaker, was hospitalized three times between ages sixteen and eighteen. He describes the experience of hospitalization as a time of confusion, boredom, and longing to get out. The adult ward on which he was placed during his second hospitalization consisted of a windowless unit with a long hallway where the patients would walk up and down for exercise: "You had the TV and the room to eat in and then you had this hallway where people would just walk up and down, and that was your day."

Heavily sedated, he spent the hours between meal times writing, playing board games, or watching TV.

"Your whole day is centered around meals, because you're not doing anything. You're not working. You're not even relaxing. You're just there. They don't know what to do with you, you're just there until you get better," he said.

After a few days of confusion following his psychotic break, Joshua figured out where he was and grew determined to get out—a challenging process.

"The thing is," he explains, "in a room full of loonies and people who are really crazy, you have no example for sanity. You have the nurses who are, like, 'Take your medicine,' and chasing after you, but there's no example for, 'Hey, you know, you should try [acting] like this to get out of the hospital.'" He later figured out that one of the men on the ward, who dressed in normal clothing and acted calmly, was actually a hospital staff member whose job was to provide an example of "normal" behavior.

After two weeks on the ward, Joshua improved enough to be let out. He says of hospitalization, "After that happens, you make it a promise to yourself that you will never go back there, because of how alienating the experience is to you and how you're removed from your life."

how you're supposed to get *better* here? Yet in our current social and medical system, hospitals are pretty much the only option available once a person is too manic, psychotic, or suicidal for their family, partner, or the general public to deal with. Some people who have been hospitalized for mental illness are traumatized by the experience; and some people feel that the hospitalization saved their life. Some people are both traumatized *and* recognize that they probably would have killed themselves if not for the hospitalization. Either way, a hospitalization for mania and depression can leave you facing two more heartbreakingly common jungle bugs:

SHAME AND DESPAIR

When you lose control of your emotions, your behavior, and/or your grip on consensus reality, you end up doing a lot things you later regret. Maybe you're embarrassed because the whole town knows you tried to jump off the bridge, or ashamed because you spent all your family's money on Italian shoes when you were manic, or feel humiliated because you were *so sure* you were finished with bipolar for good, only to be bounced back to the lowest point, the hospital, from which you now have to build up your entire life again. Maybe you feel horrible that you're going to miss a year of school while all your friends graduate, or jealous and angry that you're working on basic survival while all your friends are climbing the ladders of shiny careers. Or you're heartbroken because all your friends are getting married and having babies, and you feel like "the mental patient" who will never have all the wonderful things that "normal people" enjoy. It's not fair—you try harder than *anyone*, but somehow you're just barely making it, while all the people who don't try seem to get along just fine.

This is where people with bipolar (and other mental illnesses) have a unique challenge, as well as a unique opportunity. What is the meaning of life when an illness prevents you from doing many of the things (job, school, social achievement) your society values? What is the meaning of life when an apparent illness makes it hard for you to do the things you yourself value? To what extent is it important to cling to your goals and refuse to give up on them, and to what extent is it important to adapt to reality and accept it as it comes? Is it possible to do both?

For me, this question led me to do a lot of reading about Zen, mysticism, yoga philosophy, anthropology, nature, and other subjects. Other than being fascinating reading in and of themselves, those books led me to gently question what I assumed was important in life. Take anthropology: reading about a tiny tribe in Brazil, I was enamored by the idea of a people who spend as much time singing and dancing as working. Why was I so hard on myself that I rarely worked more than five hours a day? Oh right—it was a completely arbitrary standard imposed by industrial society. Or the Zen idea of pure presence in the moment—why did I think it was "more important" to plot out a brilliant writing career than to make a perfect cup of tea? Oh right—because my culture places a strong importance on future achievement, not presence and contentment. Slowly, slowly, I stopped worrying so much about whether I was "doing" enough or meeting the standards of a system I didn't even really believe in. I started to live in a way that made more sense to me, not a way that checked all the boxes provided by modern society.

These are not the kinds of things you can be *told* to feel or do. You sorta have to figure them out for yourself, in your own way and in your own time. Many people in our society are highly resistant to this way of thinking, because it goes against so much of what we've been taught: *hurry up, look to the future, accumulate, achieve, ascend.* But if you can manage to get past the pain and knee-jerk reactions, you will find that there are *many* meaningful ways to live, and they don't all look like being a CEO or a professor or even a person who leaves the house every day.

ONE MORE THING

One more thing about bugs, and this applies to *all* bugs: it is way too easy to get caught up in your current crisis and erroneously believe that the pain and suffering you feel now are permanent and all-pervading. But everything changes, even if it happens so slowly we spend most of our time freaking out, not believing the change is really happening at all. It is part of the nature of depression, suicidality, and even mania to make you feel like *this is the only feeling that has ever existed or will ever exist*—but it's just not true. The bugs in the jungle may be vicious, but they're insects—they *die*. Their life spans are way, way shorter than yours. Don't let them trick you into thinking otherwise.

8

THE FOREST FOR THE TREES
GETTING BACK ON YOUR FEET
AFTER MANIA OR DEPRESSION

Maybe you had to move back home from college when depression knocked you off your feet at the end of the first semester, and now you're getting ready to go back again. Or you've been doing nothing but sitting on the couch watching videos of baby monkeys ever since you were released from the hospital following your first manic episode, and you're wondering if you're ready to go back into the world and get a job. What if you crash again? What if you can't handle it? What if you can *never* handle it? Are you just going to stay on this couch watching baby monkey videos for the rest of your life?

A major manic, depressive, or psychotic episode is like when a big tree falls in the forest. There's a big, scary crash, and some of the smaller plants get crushed and the birds start hooting and tweeting and the animals scatter. The whole area looks unfamiliar: now there's this huge fallen tree with its roots in the air, and a big gaping hole in the ground. How is this ever going to look like anything other than a disaster area? Yet more quickly than you'd expect, the earth begins to reclaim the site: mushrooms and ferns appear to digest the fallen log, and flowers grow in the newly upturned soil. Eventually, there will be new bushes and trees. The forest won't be the same as it was before, but it will be healthy and bustling with life. You can be too.

PEOPLE WHO RECOVER FROM PSYCHIATRIC CRISES TEND TO SHARE SOME COMMON TRAITS:

THEY BELIEVE THAT RECOVERY IS POSSIBLE.

"I'll always be fucked up."
"It's not even worth trying."
"I'm just a mental case."
"I'm really fragile."

These are all mantras that people who recover from mental-health crises *don't* go around chanting to themselves. You are far more likely to hear them repeating these ones:

"I am going to get better."
"I am going to help other people."
"I know this experience was really meaningful, even if it hurt."
"I am going to learn so much from this."
"My life is going to be richer because I went through this."
"This experience was a big deal, but it's not going to define my whole life."

Belief is a powerful force. If you can't even imagine yourself doing something, it's far less likely that you're actually going to do it; and the things we spend time imagining have a proven effect on our ability to do them (this is why high-level athletes and musicians spend a lot of time on "mental practice," in other words, *imagining* themselves playing their best—it really does bring the reality that much closer).

At the same time, it can be hard to believe that you will recover completely if the important people in your life do not share this belief (for example, if your parents or doctor treat you like a disabled person or do not see your experience as being a relatively small part of a larger process). If this is the case, don't be afraid to talk to them about it: "Hey, I don't know if you're aware of this, but I intend to recover from this crisis, and it would help if you believed that was possible."

THEY FIND SOMETHING WORTH LIVING FOR.

It's hard to recover from *any* illness if you don't have a life worth getting better for. The ability to find meaning has been consistently identified as an important trait among survivors of all kinds of trauma. Many people who experience psychiatric emergencies find meaning in the exact crisis that knocked them off their feet (that's why so many of us go on to become psychologists, therapists, and mental-health advocates). Other people find meaning in service: to their communities, to the homeless, to the environment, or some other group or cause. Other people seek out spiritual practice. Other people find meaning in helping out their families and watching their kids grow up. The point is, the people who recover don't simply sit around trying to numb the pain or make their own lives more comfortable: they put their energy into something greater, which gives them a purpose worth living for.

THEY FIND MEANING IN THEIR EXPERIENCE.

People who *only* believe that their mania/depression/psychosis is part of an uncontrollable brain disease tend to be less healthy than people who find some greater meaning in their experience. Does this mean that everyone who has been diagnosed with bipolar or schizophrenia needs to see their experience as a spiritual experience? Of course not—but perceiving that your experience has taught you something or given you a unique perspective is much healthier than believing that you are merely the victim of a random and meaningless illness.

THEY HAVE STRONG SUPPORT FROM THEIR FAMILIES, SIGNIFICANT OTHERS, AND/OR COMMUNITIES.

A person who is hospitalized for psychosis, only to be kicked onto the street when they are deemed "stable," is going to have a far harder time recovering than a person who has a safe place to call home, loving people to support them, and other benefits like meaningful work and access to nature. This is not to say that people who come from unsupportive families or communities can't recover—it just might take a little longer, and it makes the other factors all the more important.

RECOVERY IS ABOUT WHAT'S HAPPENING NOW

Let's go back to the fallen tree example. When a tree falls, the forest doesn't try to prop it up or stick it back in its hole. Instead, the forest *incorporates* the fallen tree . . . and moves on.

In the same way, recovering from a major life event like depression or mania isn't necessarily about trying to put all the old pieces back where they were before. Even if it was possible to make everything in your life be exactly "the same" as it was before your mania or depression, it's probably not desirable. Do you really want the same life as you had when you became manic or depressed? Are there some ways in which your life could be better, or at least better adapted to what you need now?

It can take a long time (often years) to fully incorporate a life-changing experience like mania, the same way it takes years for a really big tree to decompose after it falls. Be patient. Keep observing. Even if it seems like nothing is changing, you can be sure that the tiny threads of mycelium are doing their work underground, preparing the soil for something new.

And if you're getting tired of all this hippie talk about trees, here is some more practical advice about re-entering college or the workplace following a bipolar diagnosis:

COLLEGE: A HEAVEN FOR THE MENTALLY ILL

Colleges are wonderlands of free or cheap resources that can help you find stability and sometimes meaning.

Now's the time to tax those resources for all they're worth. Your college probably has a few of the following things.

- *Free gym or swimming pool for stress relief*

  A quick swim or workout between classes is especially useful if you're depressed, because exercise boosts your energy and makes you feel good about yourself. Plus, you don't have to talk to anybody while you're doing it.

- *Free drop-in counseling*

  Some colleges have peer-counseling centers where you can drop in and talk to someone confidentially. You might feel self-conscious the first time, but remember, they're here for you—and they volunteered!

- *Free periods of extreme stress followed by periods of substance abuse and boredom*

  To keep you cycling.

- *Quiet lounges*

  My university was lounge happy. There was a women's lounge, a Native American lounge, a meditation lounge, a sustainability lounge—and most of them were massively underused. Underused lounges are the perfect place to escape from the world and grab a nap in the middle of the day, and they often have free tea and a microwave.

- *Student groups*

  Depending on the size of your university, it might have an Active Minds or Depression Bipolar Support Alliance chapter, or another group devoted to mental-health issues. A listing of good mental-health organizations can be found in the Resources section.

- *Nooks and crannies*

  Music practice rooms, library study cubicles, boat docks, and other such places offer privacy and quiet in the midst of the hectic university environment. If you need to go someplace to chill out or cry (or make out with someone), these nooks and crannies come in handy.

- *Pretty foresty stuff*

  Many university campuses have some kind of nice natural feature like a forest or pond or beach or even a garden. This makes it really convenient to catch some "green time" between classes. Hanging out with trees and plants is good for you. It can even be kind of addictive. Try it out.

- *Social network*

  The thing they don't tell you about college is that it is often one of the last chances you get to make friends and social connections before the isolating reality of "adult" life in America sets in. It is way, way harder to make friends once you're living in an apartment in some random city, working some random job than it is when you're living with roommates or in a dorm and seeing the same people in classes and social events every day. So join the poetry society and the medieval choir and the swimming club— find your people now, so that when you do have to move off-campus and get a job, you won't have to build your network from scratch.

- *Productivity and distraction*

  There's always something productive or distracting to do at a university. Crank out an essay, go to a free play or concert, or sit in on a class.

- *For people with mental illnesses, generous policies on dropping classes, changing schedules, or taking a term off*

  Universities are, by definition, progressive places. Don't be afraid to use bipolar as a medical reason for forcing your way into an afternoon class rather than an early morning one, taking fewer courses than usual, or fulfilling some of your graduation requirements online.

COLLEGE: A HELL FOR THE MENTALLY ILL

If you're dealing with a mental illness, college can be a torture palace. You can be isolated and lonely, despite being surrounded by people; overwhelmed by assignments and events; and worn ragged by the endless pressure and stimulation. When you juggle bipolar disorder with college, you might run into a few of the following:

- *Overwork*

  You have a lab report, a life-sized charcoal self-portrait, and a twenty-page essay due on Monday. What other option do you have but to stay awake all weekend to finish them?

- *Crappy schedule*

  Your first class is at 8 a.m., but your roommate likes to play death metal until 3 a.m. Your lunch break is from 3 to 3:30 p.m., and by that time you've been starving and distracted for hours.

- *Overstimulation*

  It never stops. You go to class, go to the gym, do some homework, go out for dinner with friends, go out for drinks, then go to a club and dance until it closes. Repeat three or four times a week.

- *Loneliness*

  You're hellishly depressed, but nobody in your dorm even notices that you haven't left your room in three days. You don't even know your professors' names, and you would be mortified to ask for an extension on a project.

- *Alcohol and/or drugs*

  Everyone parties all the time. You can't escape it—there's some kind of beer garden or house party or drunken grocery-cart racing every day of the week. It seems like you can't be at a social event that doesn't involve drinking.

- *Meaninglessness*

  You're studying marketing, but why?! Nobody seems to care about anything that matters. You try to join a meditation group, but they're kind of creepy. You try hanging out with the poets, but it turns out they just like to drink. There must be a friend for you somewhere, but who?

BALANCING HEAVEN AND HELL AT COLLEGE

The items in the first list should help you deal with some of the items in the second list. If overwork is driving you into hypomania, drop a class. If you're not getting enough sleep, schedule afternoon or evening classes instead of morning ones. If you need less stimulation and more alone time, take one of your classes online, so you can do it without even leaving your room. If you feel isolated, join a group and go to drop-in counseling. It's especially important to support yourself in these ways if you're returning to college after a period of hospitalization. It's not easy to go back into a demanding college environment after spending six months so doped up it took you fifteen minutes to figure out how to buy a hotel when you were playing Monopoly with your psych ward roommate. Cut yourself some slack!

CLASSES: DROP 'EM LIKE THEY'RE HOT

If you go nuts while you're in college and don't get proper documentation of your Gone Nuts status, you can end up with a ton of failed classes and maybe even screw up your chances of graduating. So make sure you get a shrink's note stating that you were unable to attend classes/exams for health reasons, and fill out any forms your university or college dean's office requires to make it official. With a note from your shrink, you can drop a class after the official drop date, defer completing an online class for a semester or two, arrange a semester off, and defer graduating until you're healthy enough to get your work done. (Other perks: free underage booze, free strippers [male strippers! lots of male strippers . . .], and all-access backstage passes. Just bring your note to Bono and tell him your psychiatrist sent you.)

In general, dropping or deferring classes and/or graduation requires a pile of forms and signatures—usually a combination of the following items.

- Medical documentation (e.g., note from your psychiatrist)
- An add/drop form with your professor's signature
- A signature from your academic advisor
- A signature from the dean

Your school registrar's office can tell you exactly which forms and signatures you need. Chasing all these people down can be a bitch, but it's even more of a bitch *not* to do it and end up with failed classes.

ALIENATION

Having an experience that alters your sense of reality can make you seriously reevaluate your life choices. The endless treadmill of reading and spitting out essays, memorizing equations, and spitting out assignments can feel meaningless—howlingly, grievously meaningless—when held up to the light of your experiences. Your eyes have been opened to a completely different worldview than that of most of your professors and classmates, and it can be hard to buckle down and think about geology when you just got back from the dark side of the moon, man.

Now and then bipolar disorder will make you slow down and ask yourself, am I living right? Are the things

I'm pursuing really worth pursuing? Do I want what I want? Do I know what I know?

Then you forget about the big questions and slip into your old patterns, until next time.

I found that the best way to deal with alienation in college was to befriend myself and to integrate my personal insights into my academic work wherever it made sense to do so. Women's Studies class? Perfect venue to write an essay about homelessness and mental-health issues among Canadian women. Eighteenth-century literature class? Edmund Burke's theory of the sublime is fascinating to consider in the light of twenty-first-century mental-hospital narratives. If your mind is constantly grappling with the idea of extreme mental states anyway, you might as well take advantage of your academic setting to explore those ideas in detail. Take whatever you find soulless and mundane and find ways to make it meaningful. Direct your powers for good instead of evil.

BE YOUR OWN MENTAL ASYLUM

Give yourself permission to drop a class, walk out of a lecture, or take a day off school if you need to in order to stay afloat mentally. The biggest mistake you can make when you're coming back to college after a breakdown is trying to do everything at once—classes, clubs, part-time job, socializing. Take it slow—three classes a semester instead of five, a house party on the weekend instead of nightly clubbing. It's better to take it easy and graduate a semester late than overload yourself and end up in the hospital, which sets you back a year.

It helps to set aside little shelters for yourself throughout the day or week. Take yourself out for coffee and have a nice, long, regrouping conversation with yourself. Skip the bar now and then and go for a walk instead. Get away from the endless hustle of campus and spend time on the beach or in the woods. Treat yourself kindly; you've just come out of an experience that's wildly out of whack with the rest of the world, and it takes time to readjust. Don't just throw yourself to the wolves. Go gently. Do it right.

THE WORKPLACE: A HEAVEN FOR THE MENTALLY ILL

Having a job can have all sorts of beneficial effects, both hidden and not so hidden, on your mood. Unless your job totally sucks, it probably provides a few of the following:

- *Steady schedule*

  Having a job with regular hours forces you to go to bed and get up at roughly the same time each day. This can be great for mood stability.

- *Social network*

  Even if you aren't best friends with your coworkers, having a job increases the number of people who know you and will notice if you're acting weird. Plus, if you don't show up for work, someone's bound to notice—always a good thing if you're prone to overdosing on sleeping pills.

- *Dollar billz*

  If you've been dependent on your parents your whole life, making money gives you a feeling of independence and self-determination you can't get any other way.

- *Meaning*

  Doing meaningful work is great for your health, especially if you can see that your work is having a visible effect on the world. If you're depressed, work can keep your mind off your emotions, and if you're hypomanic, work keeps you busy so you don't get into trouble (unless you get your hands on the staple gun).

THE WORKPLACE: A HELL FOR THE MENTALLY ILL

Work can totally mess with your system and exacerbate your mania or depression. The world is full of bitchy managers and bosses who don't give a crap about anything short of bribing the health and labor law inspectors. With any job, watch out for the following:

- *Overwork*

  Just like in college, you might find yourself overburdened with tasks and projects that stay on your mind well past working hours. Do they seriously think *one person* is enough to do the accounting for the entire corporation?

- *Crappy schedule*

  Your job starts at 6 a.m., but you can never get to sleep until 2 a.m. Or your schedule's constantly changing, and you can never establish a stable rhythm. Or you're on call twenty-four hours a day—so when the hell are you supposed to take your slumber-inducing antipsychotics?

- *Meaninglessness*

  Three months ago you realized you were the new messiah, but now you're stabilized and on meds and working at Target. Meaningful work? Ha! Mary Magdalene would weep tears of blood if she could see you now (or if you could see her—which you can't because you're not psychotic anymore. Shit!).

- *Social scumduggery*

  You're not best friends with your coworkers. In fact, they're the most obnoxious, vicious, ignorant gang of villains you've ever met. They have no idea where you're coming from and frequently make you cry. Oh yeah, and you're supposed to go out for drinks with them after work.

BALANCING HEAVEN AND HELL AT WORK

I've said it before and I'll say it again: our society is just not structured to support people who are recovering from illness or trauma, or who have different gifts and talents than the ones currently most valued by the Man. It can be really, *really* tough to hold down a "normal" job if you're more sensitive than a "normal" person or have different skills and abilities. This is not to say that people diagnosed with bipolar and other mental illnesses don't hold down plenty of normal jobs—they do—but there are also plenty of us for whom this is simply not an option.

In other ages, in other places, there were more life paths open to people who didn't fit the "normal" mold. You could be a monk or a nun, a yogi or a dervish, a priest or priestess or shaman, a warrior or a minstrel or a sage. These were respected life paths accepted by the larger society. In modern America, wandering dervishes get hassled by the cops, shamans aren't allowed to operate without a valid Shaman License, and there's just not that many places you can legally sleep without either paying rent (which requires a Normal Job) or exposing yourself to unacceptable levels of danger, harassment, or other unpleasantness.

This is a very big problem, and all I can really say is: *it's not your fault*. We are living in exceptionally hard times, and it is a tragedy of modern society that there is not a greater diversity of dignified and honorable life paths available to people. If you have trouble fitting into mainstream society, it doesn't necessarily mean you're a failure or that you are doing something wrong; to the contrary, you may be doing something very right, but society isn't equipped to recognize, much less reward it.

Other times, people with bipolar disorder do *especially* well in their careers, becoming famous actors, musicians, doctors, athletes, lawyers, and thinkers.

It might take a little longer than usual for you to find your path, and there may be more twists and turns along the way. Maybe your path will be the way of worldly success, and maybe it will be something quieter and less visible, but equally important. Don't let the (arbitrary and ever-changing) standards of society determine the value of your contribution.

SELF-EMPLOYMENT

Do you even need a traditional job? There are other ways of supporting yourself than slaving away for a boss or company that doesn't know you exist. Aren't people with bipolar more creative than usual? More resourceful than usual? More willing to take risks than usual?

If crappy jobs are a problem, why not work for yourself? You set your own schedule, choose what kind of work you take on, and develop all sorts of tasty new skills and business savvy in the process. There's no depressing office, you're nobody's bitch, and if you need to take a mental-health day, nobody can tell you otherwise.

Self-employment is a great way to dip a toe into the working world without taking on a forty-hour-a-week workload. If you are well organized and find something you love to do, it can also be a very rewarding long-term lifestyle.

Some ideas:

- Teach music lessons
- Make and sell something
- Resell stuff on eBay
- Offer a service in your field of expertise
- Freelance writing
- House-sitting
- Handyman/woman
- Massage therapy
- Gardening/landscaping
- Web design
- Computer programming
- Tutoring

MORE ADVICE FOR STAYING SANE AT WORK AND SCHOOL

If you are returning to work or school after a serious mental-health crisis, it's extra-important to develop good insight and observation skills. Don't let your desire to be a totally normal, high-functioning, productive, and efficient person get the better of you—being a star student/worker bee is not all it's cracked up to be, and it's *way* more important to feel healthy and on stable footing than to impress everybody with how many classes you can ace in a single semester. Instead of throwing yourself back into "normal" student or work life, do some experimenting. What happens when you take three classes a day? What happens if you take two classes, and spend the spare hour and a half in the forest? What happens if you go to the gym after work? What happens if you go straight home? Does a packed schedule keep you engaged and motivated, or does it lead to crashes? Does a chill schedule help you relax, or does it leave you bored and lonely? Do you get wound up when you spend too much time around people? Do you get depressed when you spend too *little* time around people? What about spending time with an animal?

Above all, don't waste time comparing yourself to "all the normal people" who can seemingly work all day, study all evening, and party all night with no ill effects (maybe they're the freaks and you're the normal one—who gets to decide these things?). What matters is how you feel, not whether you're living up to an arbitrary standard of how a person should be.

9

VOICES NOT IN YOUR HEAD
DEALING WITH FRIENDS AND FAMILY

Thanks to the wonders of genetics, there's a high chance that you have at least a couple family members as crazy as you; thanks to the wonders of assortive mating, there's a high chance that you will unconsciously seek out friends and romantic partners who are also Mentally Interesting, whether or not they have an official diagnosis. In fact, it is pretty rare to meet someone with bipolar disorder who does not have intense, brilliant, and/or troubled family members or a tendency to gravitate towards equally intense, troubled, and/or brilliant friends.

Anxious people tend to hang out with other anxious people, nerdy people tend to seek out other nerdy people, and people with intense mood states often gravitate towards equally intense partners and friends. When I scroll through a list of my favorite people and closest friends, it's hard—okay, impossible—to find a person who *doesn't* fit the category of Mentally Interesting, whether or not they've gone through the trouble of receiving an official diagnosis. The people I love most in the world are all *nuts*. And my friends who aren't nuts are nut-friendly, to the point that I've never felt any anxiety about being "different."

Family is similar. What are the odds you're the only one in your family who doesn't process the world in a totally "normal" way? Very slim! (Your family might *pretend* you're the only one, but don't let them fool you.) Sometimes, families are relieved to have a Designated Crazy Person, because it distracts from their own crazy and lets them get on with their (crazy and dysfunctional) lives, secure in the knowledge that *you* are the Problem. Other times, you might be legitimately crazier than other family members. Maybe you experienced a traumatic incident your brothers and sisters did not; maybe the combination of your mother and father's genes spawned a new kind of crazy that simply did not exist before. But trust me on this one; just because their crazy isn't as big and loud and diagnosable as yours doesn't mean it's not there.

But how do you deal with family that treats you like "the crazy one," a friend who denies your struggles altogether, or a partner who says you need treatment when you don't, or says you *don't* need treatment when you do? This chapter is all about navigating the delicate negotiations that arise when other people get involved in a Mentally Interesting life.

PART 1:
THE DATING GAME

Dating someone when you have bipolar is a lot like dating someone when you don't have bipolar, except when you have bipolar, your significant other (or S.O.) has to be cool with things like meds, depression, and occasionally being locked out of his own house at 1 a.m. while you spontaneously rewallpaper his bedroom. You also need to decide when your S.O.'s making a valid observation ("You seem manic") and when she's just using your diagnosis to score points and win arguments. A lot of the time, the fact that you have bipolar disorder will be completely unnoticeable to whoever you're dating, but for the times when it does come up, you need an S.O. who's insightful, understanding, and well informed.

"WHY IS IT SO HARD TO TELL SOMEONE I'M BIPOLAR?"

When you disclose a mental illness to someone, you get freaked out because you can't control their reaction or their image of you. You worry that they'll look at you differently, think you're stupid or weird, or that there will be an awkward silence and you'll start babbling to fill it. You take responsibility for the other person's reaction, when it's entirely out of your control. You're like a tennis player on one side of the court, trying to direct the other player's serve through telekinesis.

The truth is, you're worried for good reasons. People *do* react badly to being told somebody they are interested in (and could potentially be "stuck with" for a while) might not always be "the same person." That's a scary thought. So yeah, you might not always get the reaction you want. But the less you stress, the better it'll go.

And guess what? Hormones'll do the talking for you. People are pretty irrational. Even if it were a *terrible* idea to date you, and if they were told that every two months you turned into a bloodthirsty, evil, Satan-worshipping dragon that tore the countryside asunder and listened to tween pop, they'd probably find a way to rationalize liking you: "Well, it's only Satan." "C'mon, it's just the Jonas Brothers." If someone really likes you, they're probably going to find a way to bend this new information into *still* liking you.

Successfully telling someone about your bipolar disorder doesn't mean controlling or anticipating their reaction, but being completely comfortable with not having control. Let's say you tell your boyfriend you have bipolar, and in response he cries, vomits, and tries to roll and smoke his own underwear. So what? Eventually, that particular moment in your life will be over, and the next thing you know you'll all be laughing and getting a burrito. Or you'll decide he's neurotic and controlling and dump his sorry ass. Instead of wasting your life being freaked out and nervous, just be cool. Be cool! And realize, on every level, that if other people aren't cool, that's their problem and their choice. Freedom is nothing more than the constant, thrilling awareness that you're free, that you choose your own attitude from moment to moment—and that you can't control other people's choices.

WAYS TO MAKE YOUR BIPOLAR DISORDER EASIER ON YOUR PARTNER

- *Take care of yourself.*
  There's nothing more frustrating than watching someone who *could* be healthy and happy dig themselves into a

hole. Your partner will feel much better if he/she can tell you're taking care of yourself. So take your meds and lay off the 3 a.m. whiskey binges, already.

- *Tell them when you think you're cycling.*

  They may have already noticed—or not. If they have, they'll be relieved to know that *you know* that you're cycling and are taking steps to maintain insight. If they hadn't noticed, it can help to know they hadn't, because it tells you that you aren't way off track yet.

- *Keep other support networks current.*

  Don't stop hanging out with your friends now that you have a significant other. Keep going to your support group, your yoga class, and Sunday dinner at your aunt's house so you don't depend on your S.O. exclusively for love and support. That way when you're manic, you'll have more than one person to tell about your plan for infiltrating the White House.

- *Keep them informed.*

  Be open and forthcoming about how you're doing. Keep them in the loop about which meds you're taking and their side effects. There's no need to start a constant RSS feed about your mood states, but checking in when something comes up is reasonable. It's way less stressful to be with someone who's up front about being depressed or manic than someone who tries to hide all their feelings.

- *Be gentle.*

  Both depression and (hypo)mania can make you irritable and prone to lashing out at your partner. Take special care to be gentle with their feelings when you're depressed or (hypo)manic. And remember that they need back rubs just as much as you do.

PART 2:
FRIENDS AND FAMILY

Your friends and family are the people you eat with, gossip with, watch *Star Wars* marathons with, and generally like. They're also your most important support network. Your relationship with them goes two ways: they support you, but they also need your support. In this respect, they're not like psychiatrists. If you don't love them back, your relationship will wither. They have a vested interest in your being sane, healthy, and happy—you're more fun that way than when you're unstable and crazy. Take care of your friendships, and you'll have a much better time of life. Help your friends and family understand what bipolar is, and you'll all be able to take better care of each other.

FRIENDS AND FAMILY: KEEPING THEM INFORMED AND HAPPY

"WAS I THE LAST PERSON TO REALIZE I WAS CRAZY? DID ALL MY FRIENDS AND FAMILY KNOW IT ALL ALONG?":

Most people don't recognize the signs of mental illness. Unless you're out on the street in your boxers, muttering to yourself about aliens (and even then, some people will just think you're fun to have around at, you know, space parties and stuff), most people won't connect things like mood swings and insomnia to mental illness until you get diagnosed. And then all the little oddities they couldn't quite put their finger on "suddenly make sense." My friend started med school this year, and halfway through the first semester his roommate, who had no history of mental illness, was hospitalized for psychosis. He was shocked; he'd never seen anyone "go crazy" before and couldn't believe he'd cheerfully, cluelessly witnessed his roommate's psychosis without catching on that something was wrong or reaching out to help. Similarly, when I had my first struggles with bipolar, none of my friends recognized the signs. But when I told them the diagnosis, they said that, in hindsight, it explained a lot of things.

In the wake of a bipolar diagnosis, parents, friends, and relatives who didn't recognize the signs of mental illness are probably thinking:

"I thought he was just stressed out by exams."

"I tried to be nice to her when I saw her."

"I just thought he was drunk."

"I thought she really was pregnant with Steven Colbert's baby."

"He did always talk about a lot of weird stuff."

"I thought she was just working too hard."

"He seemed perfectly normal."

"She was always so cheerful. I can't believe she was depressed."

"If only I'd paid more attention, I could have gotten him help sooner."

"I had absolutely no idea."

Your friends and family might know less about bipolar than you think, so explain it to them. Lend them a book about bipolar. (How about this one? On second thought, don't lend. *Buy* them books. Buy *all* of them books. How about this one?) Most people who don't have one are fascinated by mental illness. They've never experienced mania or psychosis and would love to hear your stories. (Without warning, feed them high doses of magic mushrooms. Ha! Now they understand; serves them right.) Close friends often feel privileged to be offered a window into this very raw, private part of your existence. And once they understand that your depression isn't moodiness and your hypomania isn't belligerence, they won't be as hurt or confused when these happen.

You can also take a parent, friend, or significant other with you into the doctor or psychiatrist's office, so they can ask questions and feel more involved in your treatment. If you ever get hospitalized, it will be good to have a friend or parent around who knows your doctor and can help make good decisions—decisions you might be too crazy to make on your own.

Being open and well informed about bipolar yourself will make it much easier for your friends and family to be open and well informed too. If they have preconceptions of or biases against mental illness, talking about it will help them realize where and how they're wrong. You can't force people to understand, but you can leave the door open.

DEALING WITH PARENTS

Your parents' reaction to finding out you have bipolar can be more intense and harder to deal with than anyone else's. Parents get all sorts of stressed when they find out their kid has a mental illness. Guilt, anger, worry, disappointment, and overprotectiveness are just the beginning. And why not? After all, they just failed as parents, right?

Some parents are awesome; they understand, help when appropriate, back off when appropriate, stay cool.

And some parents flip their lids and suddenly look at you like you've replaced their perfect child with a demonic imposter. Instead of being mad or hurt at their reactions, try to understand where they're coming from. Maybe they need support only you can give. Maybe you need cash only they can give. It works out. Here's what they might be feeling:

- *Guilt*

  Some parents feel guilty for passing on the bipolar gene to their kids. Maybe your mom's mom had bipolar. So Mom has seen how it can mess you up, and she feels terrible for putting you at risk for it. Guilt can often masquerade as anger or resentment.

- *Anger*

  Parents who don't understand what you're going through might respond with anger: "How can you do this to us? You're such a screw-up!" They mistakenly assume that you're "doing it on purpose" or "making a scene," and might demand that you stop doing that bipolar thing the same way you tell someone to stop leaving dishes on the counter or knock off that racket in the garage. As Yoda tells us, anger is a close cousin to fear: bipolar disorder is an animal they don't recognize, they don't know what the frack they're supposed to do when they run into one, and the only surefire plan is to pick up a big stick and threaten it.

- *Worry*

  "Do you want to move back home? Should we send your big brother out there to take care of you?" Parents worry—especially if you live far away, and they can't see you to know you're OK. They worry that you're more crazy than you really are, that you can't take care of yourself, and that you'll crack without a constant supply of homemade cookies. (That last one might be true.)

- *A need to take control*

  There's nothing more annoying than being asked if you've taken your meds when you always take your meds, or being asked about your mood every day like a toddler being asked by the nanny if he's made a poo. (Side note: it's even *more* annoying being asked if you've taken your meds when you *haven't* been taking your meds. But maybe they have a point—maybe you should come down from that tree and take your meds.) Many parents turn to over-controllingness to deal with their own feelings of fear and worry in the face of your apparently "out of control" disorder.

- *Disappointment or anxiety*

  "What will this mean for medical school?" "Can you still take over the business?" "You were in the hospital through the entire football season!" "Well, call me again next semester, I guess." Parents hang a lot of hopes on their kids, and your bipolar disorder is one of those things that makes them realize your life is yours, not theirs. Just as you have to face a future of bipolar episodes, they're faced with a new set of worries about the future—some justified, some not.

Other possible aspects of parental flip-out:

- *False beliefs about bipolar*

  When people don't know much about a subject that's suddenly relevant to them, they sometimes start to pull beliefs out of thin air, or cobble together things they've heard, things they've read, and things they made up from scratch. Often this is out of a spirit of protectiveness. Let them down gently. ("Seriously, Dad, I only drive 200 mph at 3 a.m. when there's like nobody else on the road.")

- *Nonresponsiveness*

  You've reached out to them, and all you get is radio static. If you bring up your bipolar disorder, one of your parents changes the subject abruptly. "Don't they understand what a big deal this is?" you wonder.

Nonresponsiveness is probably the most confusing reaction you can get from a parent, because it gives you nothing to chew on, lean on, or even fight against. Some parents just have a hard time talking about sensitive things—or they're afraid you'll get mad if they ask you questions. The best thing you can do in this situation is to keep on being open and communicative, and not get frustrated by their perceived lack of response. Maintaining this stance is not easy, but at least it's not destructive. Some parents eventually come around and open up about it, and with others the subject of mental illness remains a closed book. In the latter case, it's especially important to find a friend or counselor with whom you can spill your guts about your moods and meds.

In order to deal with all of these reactions effectively, most parents need three things: involvement, information, and reassurance. If your parents want to feel involved in your treatment, let them go right ahead and spend hours on the phone with the health insurance company. Most moms and dads would be thrilled if their kids asked them for advice, so even if you don't take it, make your dad feel good and ask him what he does when he's depressed. If your parents are totally ignorant about what bipolar is, nurture them with information. If they worry about you constantly, throw them a bone; invite them over for dinner so they can see how happy you are, how well you're doing, and how bad a cook you are.

No matter how hysterical or inappropriate your parents' reaction is, don't let it get to you. You can only do your best to help them through your diagnosis. The rest is up to them.

"DUDE, YOU'RE ASSUMING I HAVE RELATIVELY SUPPORTIVE AND REASONABLE PARENTS. WHAT IF MY PARENTS ARE CRAZIER THAN I AM?"

This is a great question, and one that doesn't get enough attention in the bipolar literature. People with bipolar, depression, or high anxiety tend to have family members with bipolar, depression, or high anxiety—which can make an already-confusing situation even more confusing. On the one hand, it raises questions about the nature of mental illness: how much of the bipolar disorder is genetic/biological, and to what extent are the symptoms learned behaviors or coping strategies patterned on a bipolar parent?

For example, if you grew up seeing your mom repress her emotions and worry constantly about impending disasters, you might "learn" how to be anxious. If you grew up seeing your dad go on spending sprees and self-medicate with alcohol, you might "learn" this manner of coping with stress. Parents teach their kids a few things consciously ("this is how you tie your shoes!") and a *whole* lot of things unconsciously ("this is how you deal with anger—by throwing all that scumbag's furniture on the front lawn and setting it on fire!"). This second type of education is all the more effective because it is unspoken. We grow up assuming that throwing our boyfriend's furniture on the lawn is the correct and normal way of dealing with anger, and rarely stop to question why we believe this is so.

Because our families pass on so many unquestioned beliefs and behaviors, it can be extremely useful to do some serious thinking about your family dynamic and how it shaped (or continues to shape) your bipolar symptoms. How did each of your parents or guardians deal with stress? If you had to write down the unspoken "rules" of your family, especially as they pertain to emotions and stress management, what would those rules be? Here are some common ones to get you started:

"Strong people don't talk about their emotions."

"When you feel sad, the best thing to do is hide it."

"The world is a dangerous place."

"If you show any weakness, we will reject you."

"The rules don't apply to us."

"We're better than *those* people."

"Those people are better than us."

"There is nothing wrong and we are a perfect family."

"People won't like you unless you're charming and energetic."

"The best way to deal with stress is to double down and power through."

"The most important thing is to be financially successful. Relationships come second."

Can you see how these beliefs and coping strategies could contribute to mania, depression, and anxiety? Even if you *do* have a genetic predisposition to certain mood states, your beliefs and learned coping strategies have an enormous effect on the level of distress you experience from these mood states. If you believe you're "not allowed" to be sad, the experience of depression will be that much more distressing. If, on the other hand, you see the experience of sadness as normal and acceptable, you will cope much better and recover more quickly, even if it isn't exactly fun.

Having parents who are unstable or unavailable makes it that much more important to develop a strong social network—to find your own "family." This can take some doing, especially given the human tendency to surround ourselves with people who have similar problems as ourselves. (Why do smokers always hang out with other smokers? Why do people who like house music hang out with other house music fans? People, you're not going to successfully *quit* unless you find some new friends.) However, this tendency can also be an advantage: hanging out with other people who grew up with an anxious dad or a manic mom can be a great relief and an opportunity for mutual aid, as long as you are learning and not merely reinforcing old patterns.

DEALING WITH FRIENDS

Friends have slightly different needs than parents. They don't need to know if their offspring will still make it to medical school and don't want to know the names of every doctor you've seen. Your friends need a fun, cool person to hang out with—a person who cares about them as much as they care about you. How can you keep your friendships balanced when you frequently have manic or depressive episodes that need a lot of attention, and they just don't?

Most of the things I wrote about parents and significant others also apply to friends. Establish an attitude of openness about bipolar. Keep them informed and involved in your life. If they get mad at you for being manic, or feel hurt when you get depressed, understand that it's because they don't know much about mental illness. Help them learn. A friend who doesn't know anything about bipolar might think you're drunk when you're really manic, or that you're mad at them when you don't return their phone calls when you're depressed. It's easy to misinterpret these things. Be gentle with your friends' feelings, and forgive them if they misunderstand.

You're going to need to work out how much of your mood cycles to share with your friends. Do your friends need a play-by-play recap of your every depression, your every hypomanic discovery? You want to let your friends into your life, but you also don't want to be the hypochondriac uncle who calls up the whole family every time he has indigestion. It's best to find a happy medium. If your bipolar is acting up, mention it, but don't let it dominate your relationship.

REASONS YOUR BEST FRIEND MIGHT REJECT YOUR DIAGNOSIS

Now and then, you may bring up bipolar disorder with a friend or family member, only to have them roll their eyes and say, "Pffft—you're not bipolar!" (or depressed, or anxious, or eating disordered, or one-eighth Italian—tragic, I know, but it happens!). This experience can be strangely upsetting: not only did you go through the trauma of getting diagnosed with a mental illness, but now your best friend is saying you're crazy when you finally get up the nerve to tell her that a *doctor* said you were crazy, and it all becomes one big strange spiral.

Here are some reasons your best friend might question your diagnosis:

1. **She has a fixed idea of what bipolar looks like, and you're not it.**

   Definitions of mental illnesses change over time, and people don't always update their mental catalogues to keep pace with current ideas in science or culture. Therefore, your friend's mental image of a person with bipolar might be someone locked in a mental hospital for decades at a time, so heavily medicated they are unable to do much except rant and drool. Compared to this outdated idea of mental illness, you seem quite normal—so how could you possibly have bipolar?

   The problem of fixed ideas of what a given condition looks like is not unique to bipolar disorder. People who experience things like Aspergers, social anxiety, or even alcoholism sometimes encounter this problem too: "How can you be autistic? You don't memorize train schedules!" "What do you mean you're socially anxious? You seemed perfectly happy at that party!" "You're only twenty-two— there's no way you're alcoholic." It doesn't matter how much you're suffering—if it doesn't fit *their* idea of what your condition is supposed to look like, it doesn't count.

   (The same problem applies with telling your best friend you're one-eighth Italian, BTW—if you're not belting Caruso songs while holding a steaming plate of spaghetti, forget it; she won't believe you.)

2. **It's her way of standing up for you.**

   People express their loyalty in different ways. Maybe she's rejecting the diagnosis because it's her way of saying, "I've got your back!" the same way she had your back when the popular kids "diagnosed" you with being a nerd back in fifth grade: "No way, you're not a nerd. You just like interesting stuff!" (Then again, there's always a chance she's skeptical of your diagnosis because she knows you really well, and has legitimate reservations about the validity and usefulness of a bipolar diagnosis—in which case, you should be extra-glad to have her on your team!)

(Maybe your friend doesn't like Italians! Maybe she wants to protect you from the horrible, unbearable fate of being part Italian! It happens!)

3. She feels left out.

Everybody on the planet struggles; everyone on the planet suffers. But now, you have a big official word to explain your struggle, and your friend does not. Maybe it feels like you got handed a get-out-of-jail-free card—permission to be weird or to be held to different standards, or to ask for support from other people—and those perceived benefits are something she envies, even if she knows intellectually that a bipolar diagnosis comes with tons of downsides she wouldn't actually want.

("Don't mind Hilary," people say knowingly when you swing from the chandelier, "She's one-eighth Italian." But when your friend swings from the chandelier, they just get mad at her. Nooooot fair!)

4. She has a legitimate reservation about your diagnosis.

Your best friend has known you since kindergarten. She's seen you in a lotta moods, in a lotta situations. Maybe she's noticed things the doctor hasn't—like that you only get depressed after family events, or that social situations make you anxious, or that you really are a world expert on electric blankets. Instead of feeling huffy or offended that she doesn't immediately accept the bipolar label, have a conversation with her. Chances are, she has some really useful insights—insights that could help you get better faster, or to get a more accurate diagnosis if bipolar isn't the right one after all.

(PS. She knows you're not Italian, because you're Chinese, and your grandparents and great-grandparents on both sides are also Chinese. But if she's a really good friend, she'll allow that you're one-eighth Italian in spirit.)

OTHER ISSUES WITH FRIENDS AND FAMILY

Here are some other issues that can arise with relationships, both familial and romantic:

YOU FEEL LIKE THE DESIGNATED CRAZY PERSON, AND IT'S NOT FAIR.

I always find it fascinating to watch interviews with the parents of teenagers with mental illnesses, where the parent (who is clearly extremely high-strung, anxious, and more or less batshit him or herself) says piously "Oh, little Jimmy has always been so anxious! We NORMAL family members just don't know what to do with him!"

It can be very convenient to have a designated crazy person, especially if your family or partner is in denial about their own issues. It helps explain away a troubled family dynamic ("we're not troubled—he's just bipolar!") and defer attention from sensitive issues ("he wasn't abused—he just has a chemical imbalance!").

This denial can be maddening, and lots of people have spent *lots* of energy trying to change their families or make them acknowledge things they don't want to acknowledge. And while mental distress can be a wonderful catalyst for having open and caring conversations with your family, if those open conversations aren't forthcoming, there's not a whole lot you can do to force them to happen.

At the end of the day, the best thing you can do is have compassion for your family You have something they don't—you have some level of awareness and insight as to why you are struggling, while they are struggling without insight. You have an opportunity to identify your patterns and move past them, while as long as they are in denial about their patterns, they won't get to change. In this sense, being the designated crazy person can be a tremendous advantage—it's better than being the designated person-in-denial, because a crazy person has a chance at learning something, while a person who doesn't *know* they're crazy is pretty much stuck.

YOU DISAGREE ABOUT TREATMENT.

Imagination time! You've been depressed for two months. Your partner is tired of coming home every day to see you sprawled on the couch under a pile of stale burrito wrappers, in the same position as you were when she left that morning. She wants you to take antidepressants. You are determined to ride out the depression without meds. You've started fighting about it more and more. She's afraid you'll sink deeper into your rut, and you're convinced medication will turn you into a fake-happy robot just like your dad. What do you do?

Conflicts like this one can be very daunting, because the main issue (what should you do about your depression?) is often surrounded by layers and layers of fear, anxiety, and miscommunication. Both partners feel very strongly about the subject, and both have a lot at stake; both are bringing an entire lifetime of memories, beliefs, and assumptions with them. Your dad is a fake-happy robot, so you have a bad association with meds—but your girlfriend's brother refused to take medication for his severe depression and ended up committing suicide, so she has a bad association with people *not* taking meds. You both feel very strongly about your respective positions, and you both feel like you are right.

The first step in resolving this kind of conflict is to listen to your partner. Don't just pretend-listen, while quietly deciding not to budge in your position. *Really* listen. Listen with the possibility that you will end up changing your mind or shifting your position. Listen with the possibility that your partner is not just stubborn, pushy, or crazy, but actually has some valid ideas or concerns. Listen with the possibility that your partner is right.

To carry on with the depression example: you are completely right to want something more from your life than fake-happy, and to make your own decisions about powerful pharmaceutical medications. And she is completely right to want to come home to a real person, and not a defeated blob on the couch. You are not wrong, and neither is she: you're both just people, and people have fears and desires and foibles and insecurities. Not only that, but you both want the same things: to be happy, to feel loved, to have meaning in your lives. You just disagree about the best way to get there, or you have slightly different value systems that make you prioritize different things.

Now I am going to let you in on a secret: **the distress of conflicts usually comes as much from peripheral stressors like feeling misunderstood or silenced as it does from the conflict itself.** How much of your partner's distress is from you lying under a pile of burrito wrappers, and how much of it is from the fact that you won't talk to her about it, that she feels shut out and powerless, that she's afraid for the future? How much of your distress is from the threat of medication, and how much is from the feeling that she won't listen to your point of view, that she's treating you like you're unreasonable, and that your life is out of your control? If you can clear away those peripheral stressors—by communicating well, by being responsive instead of reactive—you will find that the conflict automatically becomes much smaller and more manageable.

OK, so now you're communicating openly. You see that your girlfriend's not trying to turn you into a conformist robot—she's worried that you'll go down the same road as her brother, and she feels scared and alone. And your girlfriend sees that you aren't just letting your life slide down a black hole—you're going through a dark time, and yes, you're not making the same decisions she would make, but you're being thoughtful about it, you are aware of what you are doing, and you certainly haven't given up like she feared.

What happens from this point can be very surprising. Maybe it's the first useful conversation you've had in months. Maybe once you realize you're not actually at odds with each other, you both soften a little in your point of view: she accepts the benefits of your approach, and you acknowledge the dangers. You both express greater acceptance of the other person. Maybe you ultimately go on meds and maybe you don't; but your relationship is less stressed, and neither of you feels shut out, pressured, or silenced.

NO—YOU *REALLY* DISAGREE ABOUT TREATMENT.

Imagination time! You've been psychotic for two months. Your partner is tired of coming home every day to find you roaming the streets in your bathrobe, probing tree trunks for mind-control devices. One day, you grab a knife and threaten to kill yourself; she calls the police, and you are taken to a hospital even though you maintain that you are not sick and do not need or want treatment.

In rare cases like this, your partner or family's assessment of your need for mental-health treatment is pretty much guaranteed to trump yours—not because they are morally superior, but because *you are scaring the shit out of them.* And while there are fascinating debates to be had about the rights of people experiencing severe mental illness to refuse treatment (especially when mental-health treatment in our society is so often harsh and inadequate), the fact is that if you are acting in such a way as to make people afraid that you are going to hurt yourself or them, you are going to lose your self-determination pretty quickly.

Living with a person with a severe mental illness can be almost as hard as having a severe mental illness. I'm not saying this to make anyone feel guilty—you didn't *choose* to be psychotic last winter!—but to promote a spirit of mutual understanding and compassion. If it was hard for you to be in the mental hospital for a week, think about how hard it was for your partner or family to watch you grab that knife. In short: they probably didn't have you committed because they're out to get you, but as a painful last resort. They didn't want this any more than you did.

LAST THOUGHTS ON FRIENDS,
PARENTS, AND SIGNIFICANT OTHERS

Getting diagnosed with bipolar is a great opportunity to become a more open person, a more honest person, a more caring person. Having all these people care about you makes you realize how much you value them—and how much you can return their love. If you can be open about bipolar, you can be open about other touchy things—dirty family secrets, anyone? Being "crazy" is a great excuse to speak your mind and ask awkward questions—it can even be a catalyst for taking big steps like coming out of the closet. You can use bipolar as an excuse for cracking open taboo issues in your life, and if doing so completely backfires, just blame it on the mania!

10

HIPPIE SHIT THAT ACTUALLY WORKS HERBS, WILDERNESS TIME, AND OTHER WAYS TO HELP YOURSELF

I am no anthropologist, but I do know that human beings have been around for a long, long time hunting mastodons and dancing around campfires and occasionally going through extreme mental states. Throughout most of human history, there was no such thing as a psychiatrist or a refill of Ativan—and humans developed a thousand different ways of working with mental and emotional distress, many of which are just as effective today as they were in 612 BC. Things like meditation, acupuncture, herbal remedies, and nature therapy have a long history of helping people heal their minds and bodies—and they are often gentler, safer, and more effective in the long term than "conventional" treatments for mental illness, when used wisely and correctly, with the help of experienced teachers.

Some hippie shit is just hippie shit—but some hippie shit is *good* shit, and it would be a shame to miss out on its enormous benefits simply because it seems unfamiliar at first. So let's light some incense, drink some herbal tea, and get busy. There's a whole world of healing out there.

MEDITATION

The best bumper sticker I've ever seen displays the Zen quote, "Don't just do something—sit there!"

This pretty much sums up the practice of meditation. Whether you're sitting in a monastery or yoga studio with a dozen other people or chilling out on your living room floor, meditation is all about *watching* your mind and body—not running around doing their bidding. This simple instruction, "just watch," is notoriously difficult to carry out: we want to scratch the itch or grab the chainsaw or mull over our finances or whatever. For this reason, different meditation traditions have come up with different techniques for teaching people to watch. Some traditions have you label every thought and sensation as they come up ("Noticing: desire to scratch itch. Noticing: thoughts about finances."), the same way you'd label boxes coming down a conveyor belt in a factory. Other traditions have you concentrate on breathing, or sound, or a particular color or image.

What is the point of all this sitting and watching? At its most extreme, of course, meditation is designed to bring about enlightenment (although people seem to disagree about exactly what that means). For average schmoes, however (myself included), meditation is more about helping you gain some perspective on your mind and on reality in general, so you can spend less time freaking out and more time feeling calm, content, and stable.

Different traditions phrase this in different ways, but essentially, everyone who practices meditation eventually realizes a few basic things. Thing One: nothing is permanent. Thing Two: everything changes. Thing Three: all life involves suffering. I am sure there are many important Things I am leaving out, but you can find many books and teachers who can fill in the blanks.

This knowledge of impermanence can be a great asset for people with intense moods: Is depression really forever? Are the grand plans of mania really a solution to life's problems? Consistent and gentle meditation practice can help you drive a wedge between having a manic or depressive impulse and reacting to it (so you wait five seconds before grabbing your chain saw instead of, you know, grabbing it *immediately*).

I am a total beginner and have probably said too much—so check out your local meditation center or find some good books to help you get started. Om!

FUN WITH HERBS

Some people find it fun or interesting to supplement their pharmaceutical medications with herbal remedies concocted by ancient tribes of dirty hippies and sold today at your local alternative health store. Herbs work subtly. They're not tranquilizers. Don't drink a cup of chamomile tea and expect the same effects as Klonopin. Chamomile is not Klonopin. Marijuana might be Klonopin. Klonopin might be Klonopin. But chamomile tea is chamomile tea. Appreciate herbal remedies for what they are: mild, gentle. If their effects are more of the placebo variety, that's cool. Evidence of the effectiveness of all of the following herbs is *mondo inconclusivo,* so mainly consider them a tool for tricking yourself into feeling calmer or sleepier or whatever.

Valerian might be the world's oldest insomnia remedy: the first recorded use of valerian for insomnia was in the second century. Nowadays you can find it in tea, extract, or pill form, often combined with other herbs with soothing properties, like lavender. I once found a valerian-lavender concoction you were supposed to apply to the soles of your feet. Now that's some hippie shit.

Kava kava is a beverage made of dried kava root and drunk ceremonially in Pacific islands like Samoa and Hawai'i. It's the only one of the herbs discussed here that has actually been shown in research to have a more significant effect than a placebo—namely, mild sedation and better sleep. You can get it in powder form. It doesn't exactly taste good, but it makes your lips feel numb, which is kind of cool.

Common skullcap is thought to be a mild sedative. And guess what? You can smoke it! Sweet, man!

Damiana is also thought to have sedative properties. And dig this—you can smoke it too!

St. John's wort is pretty well hyped for depression by now. You can buy commercial preparations of it in most grocery stores. It doesn't interact well with MAOI inhibitors, so don't mix your meds. And you can't smoke it. I've read that, like other antidepressants, it can induce mania or hypomania in people who have a predisposition towards those states. So definitely consult with your doctor before worting it up.

Marijuana for, um, medicinal purposes is now legal in twenty-five states. For many people with bipolar disorder, smoking a joint really is "good medicine": it can lighten depression, help you sleep, improve your appetite, and calm you down if you're edgy and hypomanic. Plus, weed has the bonus of being the one "med" that makes reggae music sound better (when's the last time lithium did that?). Like any other medicine, marijuana has different effects on different people: some people find that using it makes them more depressed, or aggravates their insomnia. And while there has been no proven link between bong-hits and bipolar, some doctors think that smoking weed makes it harder to deal with symptoms (other doctors think it's great!).

WILDERNESS TIME

I've heard that when put in survival situations, even suicidal people will fight for their lives. Some prisons dump their inmates into isolated wilderness for rehabilitation; summer camps for troubled kids and teens are also fond of this technique. Why is solitude in the wilderness so effective at sparking deep insights and life reckonings? My bet's on the fact that it pares you down to the abilities you have in your own body and your own mind. You don't have other people around to help you out or piss you off. You don't have machines or tools. You realize the extent to which your life is in your own hands—or out of them, if the weather is anything to go by.

If you have no purpose in life, going into the wilderness gives you an instant purpose: survival. Your only job, from day to day, is to take care of your basic needs for food, water, shelter, and heat, and your only company is yourself. You have plenty of time and opportunity to observe the changing nature of nature itself. You witness a sunrise and sunset every morning and evening. You see clouds forming, dropping rain, and breaking into blue sky. Your body feels keenly how the day starts out cool, warms up gradually, and cools down again as it turns to evening—something you might never feel if you spend all your time in a climate-controlled environment. If you're near the ocean, you witness the tide going in and out each day. The moon changes a little bit each night. And the plants and animals around you change visibly too. Even over the course of a single week, you can watch a seedling sprout out of its pod, a flower bloom, berries ripen, the progression of a bird's nest or beaver's dam being built.

With all this change going on around you, the wheels of your mind slow down and stop pushing forward an endless stream of concerns and mental chatter, and you're eventually forced to surrender to the fact that the world keeps on going no matter what you do.

Some people think that cities contribute to mental illness, because they're environments of intense, non-stop stimulation that can also be completely impersonal. The theory goes that the structure of a city—the primacy of motor vehicles over people, the deluge of words and images, and the endless passage of people with whom we never make eye contact or acknowledge in any way—is pathological. There's a collective fantasy of fame and urgency: you have to be someone, and you have to eat, drink, buy, or do something stimulating at all times.

You start to feel like what you do with your life is really important, when at the same time, nobody in the endless stream of strangers knows you or cares. You feel pressure to go to a show, to meet people, to entertain yourself, to be happy. Who's standing over your shoulder keeping tabs on how entertained and happy you are? This is the collective delusion of a city: that someone gives a hoot about all the rad, awesome parties you go to.

When I get depressed, I weep and feel intensely guilty for not being famous. I feel, *insanely*, that my not being famous is letting down a slew of imaginary onlookers who are very, very disappointed at my lack of progress. Fame—not marriage, money, or happiness—is the ultimate endgame. On the other side of the coin, when I'm hypomanic, I feel very optimistic that my (trivial) day-to-day activities and projects have a famous flavor to them.

Going into the wilderness dissolves this illusory fame game and reveals it for what it is: completely arbitrary. A lightning storm doesn't care how many hits a day your website gets. A prowling grizzly bear doesn't care how many people recognize you at the bar. Nature's failure to recognize you and tailor itself to your greatness breaks down your narcissism pretty fast. You realize the imaginary tally you carry around in your head has no inherent value and is completely disposable, pure ether. It's disconcerting, but ultimately the most comforting balm I know is the knowledge that I am no one. Just another green shoot rising and getting eaten by a deer. The universe swirls on.

ACUPUNCTURE

For the past couple of years, I've been going to a community acupuncture clinic for help with things like depression, insomnia, and physical pain. Community acupuncture is everything "normal" Western healthcare is not: it's affordable ($10–$30 a treatment), relaxing (treatment takes place in a dim room full of comfortable recliners) and very human (the acupuncturists wear normal clothes and act like normal people). You don't have to make an appointment weeks or months in advance, and you don't have to worry about getting a giant bill in the mail weeks later. You can realize you're having trouble in the morning and receive treatment the same day—which is extremely useful when you are trying to address symptoms in their very early stages, before they get out of hand. Because community acupuncture clinics also tend to be extremely friendly and grounding places, they can also provide an emotional boost and a calming effect completely independent of the acupuncture itself. To find a community acupuncture clinic near you, check out the People's Organization of Community Acupuncture (*www.pocacoop.com*).

ANIMAL THERAPY

Full disclosure: I never had pets growing up, and whenever I heard people talking about how their beloved Ralph or Skooter helped them get through the day, I secretly thought it was crap. But a few years ago I took home a pair of abandoned kittens I found in the park, and having finally experienced what it's like to live with warm, fuzzy animals, I've changed my Scrooge-like opinions. Animals are great, especially if you're prone to the highs and lows of a mood disorder. Having a friendly creature around helps dispel loneliness, provides structure and responsibility, and gives you a guaranteed playmate or exercise buddy. Some people with bipolar disorder even have service dogs (protected by the Americans with Disabilities Act!) who bark when it's time for meds and nuzzle them when they're having a panic attack. If you can't own a pet, try volunteering at an animal shelter or making friends with a neighbor's dog, cat, horse, pig, or llama. The love they give is definitely worth the slobber and hairballs.

MASSAGE

Sometimes, we manic-depressos get so overwhelmed by the mental anguish of depression that we forget to seek relief for our physical selves. But our bodies need relief just as much as our minds. Depression can make your head ache, your muscles tense, or your body feel completely senseless. A good massage can help you come back to life, at least temporarily. Ask your friend or lover to give you a hand, foot, shoulder, or head massage (you might have to offer a trade!). Then relax and focus on the positive physical sensations. Sometimes when I'm depressed, even paying extra attention while I brush my hair or take a shower is enough to relieve some of the mental anguish and remind myself I have a body.

This focus on the body is not just hippie shit, by the way. Studies have shown definite links between emotional pain and physical pain: being sad *hurts,* which anyone who has been severely depressed can confirm. People with bipolar disorder are more likely to experience chronic pain than the general population, and it's easy to see how being in pain can affect your mood and make positive changes more difficult—it's harder to exercise, harder to get and stay motivated, harder to resist the temptations of alcohol, TV, junk food, or other drugs. Taking care of our physical pain—by stretching, getting massages, working on body alignment, and simply becoming more aware of our bodies—is an often-overlooked piece of the mood puzzle.

GARDENING

The earth *is* an antidepressant, man. Working in a garden or rehabilitating a distressed piece of earth has dramatic effects on mood. Gardening is gently stimulating—the colors, the smells, the textures of plants and soils, the ever-changing patterns of living things. It can give you a sense of purpose (pull the weeds! give the robins a place to nest!) and feels deeply rewarding. When you tend a garden or a wild place, you can see the positive difference your work makes (try seeing the positive difference your data-entry job makes! not so easy, is it?). And if you're scientifically inclined, then yes: there is evidence to suggest that certain strains of soil bacteria trigger the release of serotonin. In other words, getting dirt under your fingernails literally makes you happy.

It is only very recently that humans have begun to spend so much of their lives indoors and have so little interaction with natural processes. Most of us aren't hunters or gatherers or even farmers; some of us don't even have a house plant to water now and then. We have heaters and air conditioners to render the weather irrelevant, electric lamps to obliterate seasonal changes in light and darkness, and our food comes from "somewhere else." On the surface it all seems very comfortable, but perhaps we aren't as well adapted to this condition as we think: our bodies respond to soil and water and trees by becoming happier and less stressed, and when's the last time you could say that about a parking lot?

VOLUNTEER WORK

Just as living indoors is a relatively recent phenomenon in human history, so is doing work that has no apparent effect on the world or apparent benefit to oneself or one's community.

Think about it: when a hunter takes a deer, she knows that deer is going to feed her community. When a medieval blacksmith makes a sword, he doesn't have to think very hard to see the purpose for what he's doing (outfitting a knight for some LARPing . . . I mean, for an authentic medieval battle!). But when many of us modern humans do our work, it just seems . . . pointless. We type numbers into machines. We write up reports about . . . something. We put plastic things into plastic boxes. It's not clear that any of this labor is helping anyone or achieving any high purpose. Modern society suffers from a distinct lack of meaningful jobs and meaningful social roles. And this is extremely depressing.

This is where volunteer work can help. Planting trees with your neighborhood habitat restoration group, serving up soup at your local shelter, helping your elderly neighbor clean out her garage, or doing any other concrete activity that has a real and verifiable effect on the world can be a great mood lifter. More abstract volunteer work, like working on climate change policy or filing freedom of information acts, can be equally powerful in giving you a sense of agency and engagement with the world. To the extent that recovery from a mental-health crisis is helped by finding meaning, volunteer work can be a faster channel than traditional employment, unless you're lucky enough to land one of those coveted Meaningful Jobs. (And hey, plenty of people have successfully transitioned their volunteer passions into Meaningful Jobs—it's just a matter of time and determination.)

Volunteer work can also help you find your tribe— other people who care about the same things you care about and see the world the same way you do. This too is a powerful protective factor against the alienation and loneliness that can accompany psychic distress.

DEEP BREATHING

Deep breathing is one of those things you hear about so often it just seems like a cliché: "Deep breathing? Oh yeah, you and Oprah and my annoying New Age aunt are always going on about that . . . whatever." But pretty much every meditation tradition works with the breath, and for good reason: breathing deeply triggers a relaxation response as surely and automatically as banging your knee with a hammer triggers a knee-jerk response. In other words, if you breathe deeply, you are *going* to relax—you physically won't be able to help it. I don't know about you, but this kind of guarantee works really well for me. I like knowing that this is something I can't screw up; it's built into my body. Breathe deeply, and you *will* relax, even if you don't change anything else about what you're doing or where you are or what's going on around you.

PSYCHEDELICS

Psychedelics exist. Plenty of people take them. There's no point pretending that people with mental illnesses don't take them. Yet it's practically impossible to find good information about psychedelics and bipolar disorder because everyone who writes a book or puts up a website has to decorate their information with more disclaimers than a Christmas tree has twinkle lights, just to cover their backs. You find the kind of ambiguous statement like, "I'm bipolar and shrooms work great for me and heal my depression. But you should never, ever drop shrooms if you're bipolar because they can trigger shit in your brain that will screw you up permanently." Well, will they or won't they? Is taking psychedelics riskier for people with bipolar, because our brain chemistry is easily triggered into episodes, or are people with bipolar better equipped to take psychedelics than the general population, because we're already experienced navigators of alternate realities? So-called studies on the subject are no better than subjective accounts. Everyone's hands are tied.

The only conclusions I can draw after hours of research are that psychedelics might have a bad interaction with your meds, and they may or may not trigger a psychotic, depressive, or manic episode. Real helpful, right?

Experienced trippers say the most important thing about taking psychedelics is being stable, able to keep your cool, and in the right setting—*not* whether or not you have a diagnosis. The most important thing about being able to drive a fire truck is being calm, alert, and well trained in fire-truck driving—qualities a person with bipolar can possess as easily as a person without. When making the decision to drop or not to drop, evaluate yourself thoroughly and honestly: What are your abilities, your state of mind, your personal history and current level of stability? Is this a good time to risk triggering an episode? Have you taken this kind of mushroom/cactus/button before? Do your best to research whether or not there's a danger of nasty interactions with whatever meds you're on. And if in doubt, don't do it. Doubt and apprehension guarantee a bad trip.

I'm not experienced enough with psychedelics to give any more advice on the subject or wax poetic about how the fractal kingdom expanded my mind beyond the limits of reality. I know people with bipolar disorder who dose regularly and seem completely fine and unaffected, and people with bipolar disorder whose psychedelic use temporarily made their lives a living hell. There doesn't seem to be a single rule.

P.S. Excessive rumination about whether a drug will "screw you up for life" can give the experience more import and drama than it really deserves. Every day, all kinds of people take shrooms and acid and peyote and whatnot. Normal people, mundane people, just boring ol' people. Fifteen-year-old high schoolers and thirty-year-old ski instructors. Your history prof. All around the world, people who have taken psychedelic drugs are turning out OK, turning out to be losers, turning out to be successful, turning out to be psychotic—the whole range. What's the big deal? You're just another grain of sand on a vast beach. Sooner or later even the most impactful psychedelic experience fades into kitsch. So chill out.

CONCLUSION

GIFTS FROM THE JUNGLE

People who go through extreme experiences of any kind tend to bring back unique skills, insights, and gifts from the other side. The jungle isn't just full of poisonous snakes and spiders; there's cool stuff in there too. If this book were a movie, we would be at the point at which the heros and heroines, having trekked through a jungle sometimes perilous and sometimes magical, having frolicked in hidden waterfalls, having dreamed potent dreams and eaten mashed bugs for breakfast, now emerge at a high clearing from which they have a long and breathtaking view. The landscape is spread out all around them, with rivers winding through it and flocks of birds wheeling above it. While there is still plenty of new and unpredictable jungle to be explored on the journey ahead, our protagonists feel, deep within their bones, that they are strong and clever and patient enough to tackle any setback or recognize any opportunity.

They look with fondness and self-compassion at their mistakes (that time we ate the red-capped mushrooms and spent three days vomiting!) and with appreciation at the wisdom they gained along the way (leopards make a scary screech but rarely attack, and you can travel safely in their territory). They mourn their lost companions and celebrate their new mentors, helpers, and friends. Above all, they vow to always be of service to any newcomers they encounter in the jungle—the young and frightened, the lost and panicked, the sick and injured, the lonely and confused.

Over the years, I've had the good fortune to meet hundreds of people diagnosed with bipolar, and have observed certain traits that many seasoned jungle wanderers seem to possess:

EMPATHY

Jungle wanderers know what it feels like to be so sad you want to die, or so dazzlingly *aware* you can feel the rustling of every individual leaf on a tree. They know what it's like to struggle with work or school or family life, or to go through serious challenges like homelessness, imprisonment, or hospitalization. They know that there is more to every person's story than meets the eye, and for that reason, they are quick to listen and slow to judge.

PERSPECTIVE

Jungle wanderers know that life is long and contains infinite possibility. They know that things that seem important in the short term are often less important in the long term; that setbacks can have hidden gifts and that successes can contain hidden setbacks; and that the ingredients for a meaningful life are not always what they tell you in school. They often use this perspective to help other people going through the jungle for the first time.

CREATIVITY

Jungle wanderers are artists, musicians, dancers, writers, and thinkers, even if they only show their talents to a small circle of people, or even practice them alone. They have access to deep wells of experience and emotion that they channel into their creative practices.

VISION

Jungle wanderers are environmentalists, social justice activists, and advocates for vulnerable people and places. They know the world is upside down and backwards in a million different ways, and they make it their life's work to fix a piece of it, even if it's small.

———◆———

Reader, I am so grateful that we have been able to take this trip together. Mental health is an endlessly fascinating subject, and I feel lucky to have been given the opportunity to do some tramping around a few of its canyons, although there is still so much territory I hope to someday ponder and examine. Fellow travelers, I am with you through the 3:00 a.m. breakdowns and the all night flights of fancy, the weeping and the huzzahs, the grand plans and the complicated realities. May we all continue to listen more deeply and observe more clearly, examining this thing called the mind through a million different angles and more.

Here's wishing you a life of adventure, friendship, and meaning. Take care of each other,

Hilary

RESOURCES

THE ICARUS PROJECT

www.theicarusproject.net

The Icarus Project is the biggest, most well-organized mad pride organization you can find on the Internet. Its mantra is "navigating the space between brilliance and madness." Its website has articles, forums, and community resources for mental health.

CRAZYMEDS

www.crazymeds.us

Crazymeds is the place to go for exhaustive information on the meds you're taking. The site is run by Jerod Poore, a "citizen medical expert" who himself has autism and bipolar disorder. In addition to regularly updated drug info, there are message boards where you can connect with other people who take crazy meds.

NATIONAL INSTITUTE OF MENTAL HEALTH (NIMH)

www.nimh.nih.gov

NIMH is a government-funded organization that publishes news and research on mental-health topics. It's a good place to read about the latest clinical trials or the results of studies about bipolar, schizophrenia, and depression. Keep it in mind for your next research paper.

MAD IN AMERICA

www.madinamerica.com

Mad in America is a website founded by Robert Whitakre, former director of publications at Harvard Medical School. It publishes up-to-date articles and blog posts by researchers who are exploring approaches to mental-health treatment that go beyond medication: "We believe that this mix of journalism, education and societal discussion can provide the seed for a much-needed remaking of mental health care in the United States. It is evident that our current 'brain disease' model is flawed in so many ways, and we believe that it needs to be replaced by a model that emphasizes our common humanity, and promotes robust, long-term recovery and wellness."

MADNESS RADIO

www.madnessradio.net

"An hour-long interview format, Madness Radio focuses on personal experiences of 'madness' and extreme states of consciousness from beyond conventional perspectives and mainstream treatments. Madness Radio also features authors, advocates, and researchers on madness-related topics, including civil rights, science, policy reform, holistic health, history, and art."

HARM REDUCTION GUIDE TO COMING OFF PSYCHIATRIC MEDS AND WITHDRAWAL

www.willhall.net/comingoffmeds

An excellent, compassionate, and well-researched guide to—you guessed it—tapering off psychiatric medication, written by Will Hall in conjunction with the Icarus Project: "A 'harm reduction' approach means not being pro- or anti- medication, but supporting people where they are at to make their own decisions, balancing the risks and benefits involved."

RECOMMENDED READING

Allen, Frances. *Saving Normal: An Insider's Revolt Against Out-of-Control Psychiatric Diagnosis, DSM-5, Big Pharma, and the Medicalization of Ordinary Life.* New York: William Morrow Paperbacks, 2014.

Antonetta, Suzanne. *A Mind Apart: Travels in a Neurodiverse World.* New York: Tarcher, 2005.

Earley, Pete. *Crazy: A Father's Search Through Mental Health Care Madness.* New York: Berkley, 2007.

Greenberg, Gary. *The Book of Woe: The DSM and the Unmaking of Psychiatry.* New York: Blue Rider Press, 2013.

Hillman, James, and Ventura, Michael. *We've Had a Hundred Years of Psychotherapy and the World is Getting Worse.* New York: HarperOne, 1993.

Jamison, Kay Redfield. *An Unquiet Mind: A Memoir of Moods and Madness.* New York: Vintage Books, 1996.

————. *Touched with Fire: Manic-Depressive Illness and the Creative Temperament.* New York: The Free Press, 1993.

Macy, Joanna, and Johnstone, Chris. *Active Hope: How to Face the Mess We're In Without Going Crazy.* Novato, CA: New World Library, 2012.

Mator, Gabe. *When the Body Says No: Exploring the Stress-Disease Connection.* Hoboken, NJ: Wiley, 2011.

Nakazawa, Donna Jackson. *Childhood Disrupted: How Your Biography Becomes Your Biology, And How You Can Heal.* New York: Atria Books, 2015.

Whitakre, Robert. *Mad in America: Bad Science, Bad Medicine, and the Enduring Mistreatment of the Mentally Ill.* New York: Basic Books, 2010.

NATIONAL CRISIS HOTLINES

NATIONAL SUICIDE PREVENTION LIFELINE

1-800-273-TALK

National 24/7 suicide crisis hotline. Call for free from any phone, any time, to speak with a trained counselor. Your call will be routed to the closest crisis center in your area, and whoever you talk to will be able to direct you to further help once the call is over. Also available in Spanish.

NATIONAL RUNAWAY SWITCHBOARD

1-800-RUNAWAY

If you're between the ages of twelve and twenty and have run away from home (for example, during a manic episode), you can call this number to arrange a free Greyhound ride back to your folks. The switchboard operators will also connect you with resources and counseling if your family is having conflicts.

ABOUT THE AUTHOR

Photo © Gabriel Jacobs

Hilary Smith is the author of the novels *Wild Awake* and *A Sense of the Infinite,* both from HarperCollins. She lives on an off-the-grid homestead near Nevada City, California, where she writes, practices music, and tends the land.